Jeremy Oliver's
Good Wine Guide 2017

Woodslane Press Pty Ltd
10 Apollo Street
Warriewood, NSW 2102
Email: info@woodslane.com.au
Tel: 02 8445 2300 Website: www.woodslane.com.au

First published in Australia in 2016 by Woodslane Press
© 2016 Woodslane Press, text © 2016 Jeremy Oliver, images © as indicated
This work is copyright. All rights reserved. Apart from any fair dealing for the purposes of study, research or review, as permitted under Australian copyright law, no part of this publication may be reproduced, distributed, or transmitted in any other form or by any means, including photocopying, recording, or other electronic or mechanical methods, without the prior written permission of the publisher. For permission requests, write to the publisher, addressed "Attention: Permissions Coordinator", at the address above.

The information in this publication is based upon the current state of commercial and industry practice and the general circumstances as at the date of publication. Every effort has been made to obtain permissions relating to information reproduced in this publication. The publisher makes no representations as to the accuracy, reliability or completeness of the information contained in this publication. To the extent permitted by law, the publisher excludes all conditions, warranties and other obligations in relation to the supply of this publication and otherwise limits its liability to the recommended retail price. In no circumstances will the publisher be liable to any third party for any consequential loss or damage suffered by any person resulting in any way from the use or reliance on this publication or any part of it. Any opinions and advice contained in the publication are offered solely in pursuance of the author's and publisher's intention to provide information, and have not been specifically sought.

National Library of Australia Cataloguing-in-Publication entry

Creator: Oliver, Jeremy, 1961- author.
Title: Australian wine guide 2017 : your guide to selecting, enjoying and cellaring Australian wine /Jeremy Oliver.

ISBN: 9781925403503 (paperback)
Notes: Includes index.
Subjects: Wine and wine making--Australia--Guidebooks. Wineries--Australia--Guidebooks. Wine--Storage--Guidebooks.
Dewey Number: 641.220994

Printed in Australia by McPhersons
Book design by Christine Schiedel

Good Wine Guide 2017

Jeremy Oliver

is one of Australia's foremost wine writers and its leading wine presenter. A widely read and fully independent wine commentator, Jeremy was named the inaugural Wine Writer of the Year by the widely circulated Australian Wine Selector magazine. Jeremy is also seen on Australian television and hosts China's most popular online wine TV series.

A trained winemaker, Jeremy is known for his honesty and the integrity of his opinion. He is the author of nearly 30 books and his best-selling The Australian Wine Annual, shortly to celebrate its 20th edition, is translated into Mandarin Chinese each year. With the publication of Enjoying Wine with Jeremy in Mandarin in 2008, Jeremy became the first western wine author to write and publish a wine book for the Chinese market in its own language.

Jeremy contributes to numerous national and overseas publications and regularly appears on a number of international TV networks. He is the founding presenter of Winevine.tv, a new international TV network devoted to wine and has made hundreds of other appearances on radio and television.

Born in late 1961 at Ballarat in western Victoria, Jeremy Oliver was educated in Australia and England. By the time he completed a Bachelor of Agricultural Science at the University of Melbourne he had decided to pursue a career with wine. After a year in Coonawarra, during which he worked firstly at Lindemans and then at Katnook Estate, he studied winemaking at Roseworthy College as a postgraduate in 1984. That year, aged 23, he published his first book, Thirst For Knowledge, becoming the world's youngest-ever published wine author.

Today he remains as enthusiastic as ever about connecting Australians with their wine and supporting Wine Brand Australia around the world. He operates the website **jeremyoliver.com**.

Many thanks to ROBIN SHAW, Australia's foremost expert in wine tourism, who has contributed the cellar door content to this book. The founder and operator of Wine Tourism Australia, Robin has worked with hundreds of cellar door operations in Australia and other countries to improve the visitor experience they offer.

My sincere thanks to David Scott and Andrew Swaffer of Woodslane for embarking on this project and contributing to its shape and form. Thanks also to designer Christine Schiedel for her breezy layout and my wife, Jennifer Oliver, for rounding up hundreds of wines, labels and images.

All the photographs are copyright and may not be reproduced without permission. All the images, except for wine labels, are © and courtesy of Wine Australia, Wine Tasmania, Chad Elson, Rebecca Appleton, Zoe Lane, Alicia Bennett, Andrew Koerner, Nathan Kinzbrunner, David Reist, Frances Andrijich, Tim Jones / Wine Australia and others. My thanks to these friends and colleagues for supplying the photography that brings this book to life. The wine labels are © the individual wine producers.

CONTENTS

2	Australian wine in 2017
12	Grape varieties and styles
52	Where wine is grown in Australia
124	Pairing wine with food
131	Best wines to enjoy by occasion
148	The Jeremy Oliver Wine Awards: the best buys in 2017
158	How wine is grown and made
171	Enjoying and handling wine

Australian WINE IN 2017

THE BASICS

WHAT IS WINE?

Who**ever** you are, wine for you is something entirely different and unique. It might be something you drink without thinking: a mere alcoholic beverage that might be more palatable to you than beer or spirits. Perhaps, like many Europeans, you might think of wine as a food: you drink it every day while you are dining with friends or family, and you don't give it a second thought. Or it might have become a professional tool: something you think you need to master on your climb up the corporate ladder.

You might also find wine interesting and pleasurable enough to have some favourite examples. Or wine might have become your hobby, a genuine interest bordering on fascination – so you taste wine regularly, read about it often and talk about it all the time. It might even become your obsession, which might alarm your friends unless, of course, they happen to share it!

Whatever it is to you, wine is an increasing part of the lives of a growing number of people all over the world. It is perhaps an epitome of the finer aspects of the western lifestyle, but in truth it is just as much at home today in Asia and the Middle East. Wine has become a universal language and a point of connection for people who might not otherwise have that much in common. It breaks down barriers, crosses borders and offers its own surprises and challenges. It is a connection to the earliest recorded human civilizations, yet its great fascination lies in the future. Who will make the great wines next year, and where will they make them? What new regions will be unearthed? For how long will the best bottles last? And what will those wines reveal when they reach the peaks of their journeys?

WINE HAS SERVED

over the millennia as inspiration to poets, authors, composers and artists alike. A medicine of ages past and present, wine has been described as bottled sunlight, the flower in the buttonhole of civilisation, the most civilised thing in the world. According to Louis Pasteur: 'A meal without wine is like a day without sunshine'. You can be forgiven for ignoring this advice at breakfast!

Wine is art and wine is science. Like all art, wine can be admired for its more obvious effect on the senses, in this case appearance, scent and flavour. But, like art that can be appreciated intelligently, the variations of colour, bouquet and flavour that give wine its character and subtlety are often the cause of long and animated conversation. More than ever, science now provides the foundation upon which winemakers and growers can indulge their artistic flair and talents. Science also often provides the answers when nature's challenges (such as difficult seasons and obstinate ferments) tests a producer's ability to create a wine of an expected standard.

The relaxing, stimulating and enlivening properties of wine can be experienced after two or three glasses. It has been proven that moderate wine consumption reduces the incidence of coronary disease, prolongs life, provides rare (but significant) levels of vitamins and minerals, increases mineral adsorption, aids digestion and relieves tension. It will neither induce brain damage nor upset pregnancies or births when enjoyed in moderate amounts.

Wine provokes our imaginative facilities into action, and may rightly share the credit or blame for some of our more outrageous efforts. While other beverages and concoctions strive for consistency, part of wine's fascination lies in its immense variation. Wines from different vineyards, years, winemakers, cellars, varieties, when paired with different foods and cellared for different lengths of time all taste... different. If you wish to, you can never, ever stop learning about it. The enjoyment of wine is a journey of your own style, passion and duration.

AUSTRALIA'S PLACE IN THE WORLD OF WINE

*A*ustralia has been making wine since the first Governor of the State of New South Wales planted the continent's first vineyard in 1791. In the century that followed, Australia became a significant exporter of wine to Europe and the United States. The trigger that led to a major decline in Australian winemaking was the global depression that began in 1893, ultimately leading to the First World War.

It is really after the Second World War that the Australian wine industry came to resemble what exists today. Australia had not really been a wine-drinking country for several generations, but Australian soldiers who had fought in European

AUSTRALIAN WINE

is almost as diverse as the county's own population. There are more than 2500 wineries in Australia in around 100 different wine regions, of which about 70 have been officially recognised. Australia in 2016 has more than 170,000 hectares of vineyards and with sales to more than 100 countries is the world's fourth largest wine exporter.

countries brought back with them a taste for wine and a continental lifestyle. Furthermore, the subsequent immigration to Australia of large numbers of Italian, Greek and northern European peoples helped create a demand for wine in this country.

Modern Australian cities are extremely multicultural, with the presence of dozens of different nationalities, most of which have retained their gastronomic traditions. The streets of Australia's capital cities are populated by restaurants representing many of these cuisines and wine, local and imported, is a regular part of the dining experience they offer.

It was only around twenty years ago that Australia took itself seriously as a wine exporter. Today, Australia's export success has redefined the way the world looks at wine. Based on a system that encourages both flexibility and accountability, Australia's success in marketing its inexpensive and flavoursome varietal wines through its skill at developing and promoting international brands is a modern marketing phenomenon. Names like Penfolds, Jacob's Creek, Hardy's and YellowTail are instantly recognised wherever wine is enjoyed.

To some extent, Australia's phenomenal international success with inexpensive branded wine has concealed from many export markets its ability to create wines that genuinely reflect the identity of their regions and sites. While Australia's iconic collection of premium wines like Penfolds' Grange, Henschke's Hill of Grace and Giaconda's Chardonnay have well-established international reputations, makers and marketers of Australian wine are now keenly focused on this challenge.

Australia's new focus is towards its increased awareness of what makes it different and unique. It is working harder than ever before to promote its finest regional and individual vineyard wines around the world and has found large and welcoming markets in Asian countries like China, Taiwan, Japan, Korea and Hong Kong.

Australia's environment is largely unpolluted and clean. Its viticulturists have been steadily phasing out, and in some cases eliminating the application of chemicals in vineyards as part of the trend towards a more organic system of growing grapes. The Australian wine industry, which also depends on the challenging climate of the world's driest continent, is also committed towards an environmentally responsible and sustainable future.

AUSTRALIA MAKES THE BEST AUSTRALIAN WINE IN THE WORLD

and for many wine buyers around the world this is something to be savoured. To a large extent, however, the Australian wine industry has lacked the confidence to make the best possible wine it can. Recently this pendulum has started to swing back in a very positive direction and Australia is now making a higher proportion of the world's best wine than ever before.

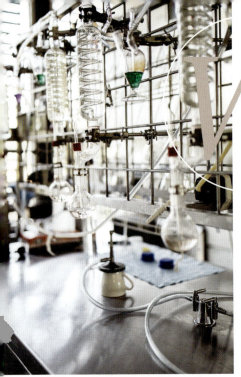

WINE PLUS KNOWLEDGE EQUALS ENJOYMENT

While you are the only person who can determine how much you want to know about wine, there is no doubt that the more you learn about it, the more you will inevitably enjoy wine. You can't expect the fascinations and the intricacies of wine to make themselves apparent to you without learning how to identify them for what they are. We can all do it, but it takes a little time…

One of the comments I hear most often from the wine-drinking public is 'I might not know much about wine, but I know what I like'. While it is polite for me to agree with those who say that, it would also be quite easy to argue with them. How do they know, without much knowledge – and therefore experience – what they actually like? How do they know there are not hundreds of wines that they might actually prefer to those they choose every day out of sheer habit and fear that they might leave their own comfort zones?

There is nothing to be embarrassed about if you don't know much about wine, but I reckon I'm living proof that the more you do know about it, the more fun it will give you. And, having been writing about it for thirty-plus years, I am delighted to be able to say that I have never, ever been bored with it! With a little knowledge, you can match wine to your food, your mood and your budget. You can match it to the enthusiasm and knowledge of your friends. You can even match it to music!

I try to make an honest effort to understand those of us who choose

THIS BOOK IS ALL ABOUT

lighting up a way towards wine knowledge and enjoyment, but in a user-friendly and approachable way. It is possible to be knowledgeable about wine and still be humble and normal. There's no reason why wine should turn anybody into a raving snob, although God knows, it certainly does from time to time. But it's not the wine's fault!

not to drink and enjoy wine, even though genuine health-based reasons for this are few and far between. But in this I fail miserably. I just don't get it. Why, when wine is so affordable, so accessible and in moderation so healthy, would anyone decide not to enjoy it?

The goal of this book is to introduce you to wine in general and Australian wine in particular. It introduces you to Australia's best wine regions, its leading grape varieties and its best cellar doors. It takes you through how wine is grown and made, how it is cellared and served. All the way through, it shows you the best wines to buy – as examples of regions or varieties, or just as great wines to have near to hand for virtually any occasion.

Jeremy Oliver's Good Wine Guide is the ideal start for your journey with wine.

Bon voyage!

MAJOR GRAPE VARIETIES IN AUSTRALIA

Throughout the centuries, different grape varieties have been selected and refined by winegrowers and makers to create wines that best reflect the individuality and character of their regions of origin. There are many hundreds of different grape varieties native to different parts of Europe and the Middle East, but only a relative handful are today known around the world as the premier or 'noble' varieties. These varieties typically develop a powerful synergy with their regions, so they actually become an integral part of their regions' identity.

For example, we mainly associate the French region of Bordeaux with cabernet sauvignon and merlot, the Italian region of Chianti with sangiovese, the Mosel River in Germany with riesling and Burgundy, also in France, with chardonnay and pinot noir.

Grape varieties have been selected for their special, repeatable expression of their characteristic scents, flavours and textures, which have been refined over the centuries. While virtually all wine is made from the same species of European grapevine (vitis vinifera), the differences between these varieties can be likened to the differences we know and understand between the different kinds of apple we might buy at a grocer.

Furthermore, provided they are grown in a moderately sympathetic environment, these varieties will reproduce their characteristic flavours and textures in an identifiable way wherever they are grown. In other words, once you know what a chardonnay tastes like, you should know broadly what to expect from a wine labelled as 'Chardonnay' whether it might have been made in Australia, the US, Chile or wherever.

It takes time, however, for growers and makers in younger wine making countries like Australia to determine

MATCHING VARIETIES WITH REGIONS

As you learn more about wine you'll notice that wine regions tend to specialise in certain grape varieties – hopefully the ones that grow best in each. Typically, as new regions are opened up by what are typically quite intrepid growers, they will plant a range of different grapes to test for themselves which are going to perform best over the long term.

Trouble is, it can take around five years before a new vineyard can produce a wine that will deliver this kind of assurance or not with some certainty. So we resort to science and history.

Different grape varieties typically ripen at different times of the season, being at the extremes either 'early ripening' or 'late ripening'. The earlier-ripening grapes – chardonnay and pinot noir being two fine examples – therefore don't require as much sunshine to ripen their grapes as a late-ripening variety like cabernet sauvignon. That's why the cooler regions, typically found in the south of this country or else at an altitude high enough to be cooler than the surrounding lands (such as the Adelaide Hills and Orange), typically produce finer wines from the earlier-ripening varieties than their warmer counterparts. Similarly, however, the coolest of Australia's wine regions are typically too cold to regularly and reliably ripen varieties like cabernet sauvignon and petit verdot.

Other factors like soil type, drainage and aspect will influence the precise choice of which variety is planted in which vineyard.

The historical component is to study which grape varieties typically produce the most famous and sought-after wines from any given region. It can take some time for the growers and makers within new wine regions to focus collectively on a small number of varieties, but you will see that long-established high-quality regions are typically known for long-established relationships with certain grape varieties, simply because they have stood the test of time and are still relevant in the modern wine market today.

Some well-know examples of this kind of synergy are Coonawarra with cabernet sauvignon, the Hunter Valley with semillon, the Eden Valley and Clare Valley regions of South Australia with riesling and the Yarra Valley and Mornington Peninsula regions of Victoria with pinot noir.

As you journey through this book you will become more familiar with the better combinations of regions and varieties, with plenty of examples of recommended wines to try. It's important to learn some of the best regions for your favourite wine varieties, just as it is to learn what to expect should you head off to explore a new wine region.

which varieties are best suited to which regions, since in many cases there is no prior history of grape growing to provide clear-cut answers. Australia has been making wine for two centuries, but many of its most prestigious and exciting regions are only three decades old. After that short time we can already enjoy the special associations and synergies evident between certain grape varieties and wine regions.

The next pages will introduce you, variety by variety, to the key winegrapes that are most important to modern Australian wine.

THE WHITE VARIETIES

Arneis

Originating in the hills of Roero in the famous Italian region of Piedmont, arneis is today becoming popular in the cooler regions of Victoria, Tasmania and South Australia, especially the Mornington Peninsula and the King Valley (both Victoria) – which has become such a home for Italian varieties in Australia. A white variety, its wines are typically rich, round and dry, with a characteristic presence of pear, apple and apricot flavours. As they age, it wines become more nutty and honeyed. They finish with a soft, but distinctive acidity. Some makers are experimenting by blending it with other white Italian varieties.

Arneis isn't really a variety to cellar, so the maximum time I'd leave an example of this wine would be about two to three years. Typically, it's best enjoyed while still young and brisk.

Crittenden Estate Oggi White Blend 2015
Mornington Peninsula
$30-$49
89/100
Honeyed stonefruit and pear flavours, smooth and savoury.

Bird in Hand Arneis 2015
Adelaide Hills
$20-$29
90/100
Fresh apple, pear and melon flavours, smooth and refreshing.

Holm Oak Arneis 2016
Tamar Valley
$20-$29
88/100
Pungent and meaty, with rich melon, pear and apple flavour.

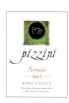

Pizzini Arneis 2016
King Valley
$20-$29
89/100
Fragrant and spicy, with faintly candied gooseberry and guava flavour.

YarraLoch Single Vineyard Arneis 2012
Yarra Valley
$20-$29
91/100
Taut and fresh, with pristine pear and green tea notes.

Chardonnay

The classic white grape from Burgundy (France) has become one of the most popular around the world. Its wines range from tight, austere expressions from cooler climates to juicier, riper and almost oilier styles from warm to hot regions. When grown in cool regions its wines are lightly scented and lightly spicy, with flavours of pear, apple and white peach. Warmer climate chardonnays are suggestive more of nectarine, melon, tropical fruit and citrus, and finish with softer, more gentle acids than the more crisp, focused and mineral wines from cooler sites.

Today chardonnay has fully recovered from its unfortunate years a decade and more ago in which its wines were flat, flabby and over-oaked. Today most Australian chardonnay is vibrant and fruit-driven, with mouthfilling flavours wrapped in a refreshing level of acidity.

The better chardonnays are usually fermented and then aged for up to a year in oak barrels to further develop their structure and complexity. Because it typically needs to be enhanced by

Castle Rock Estate Great Southern Chardonnay 2015
Great Southern
$20-$29
90/100
Tropical and citrus, long and tangy.

Climbing Chardonnay 2015
Orange
$20-$29
90/100
Developing, dry and savoury; long and nutty.

Coldstream Hills Chardonnay 2015
Yarra Valley
$30-$49
94/100
Pristine and spicy with refreshing acids.

Delamere Chardonnay 2014
Pipers River
$30-$49
94/100
Smoky and nutty, with delicious stonefruit flavour.

Heemskerk Coal River Valley Chardonnay 2014
Coal River Valley
$30-$49
94/100
Long and shapely, wild and mineral.

the addition of winemaking-derived flavours and textures, it's a variety that allows winemakers to express their own individuality and preference for style.

While inexpensive chardonnays are at their most attractive while relatively young, chardonnay can develop significant richness and weight with cellaring. However, you would only keep the very finest chardonnays for longer than five years.

Although most chardonnay grown in Australia finds its way into a bottle of dry white, a significant proportion is used to make sparkling wine.

Killerby Chardonnay 2014

Margaret River

$20-$29

93/100

Smooth, creamy and smoky, with generous fruit.

Seppelt Jaluka Chardonnay 2015

Henty

$20-$29

94/100

Nutty, spicy, mineral and savoury; very laid-back.

Seville Estate Chardonnay 2015

Yarra Valley

$30-$49

94/100

Elegant, savoury, long and finely balanced.

Stella Bella Chardonnay 2015

Margaret River

$20-$29

91/100

Citrus and tropical fruits; long and crystalline.

Stonier Lyncroft Vineyard Chardonnay 2014

Mornington Peninsula

$30-$49

95/100

Elegant, smooth and creamy, with bright citrus and tropical flavours laced with spice.

Chenin Blanc

Chenin Blanc originates in France's Loire Valley. Its wines are full in fruit and generous in flavour, with a perfumed, peachy aspect and a typical herbaceous edge. Some chenin blancs are bottled with a little sweetness. They typically mature quite quickly, becoming very honeyed and toasty, while the best are still able to retain freshness and vitality. Most of Australia's chenin blanc is made in a mouthfilling, faintly herbal style without oak. Peel Estate in Western Australia has made a speciality of a fuller, rounder oak-matured style.

Amberley Chenin Blanc 2015
Western Australia
$12-$19
83/100
Sweet and tropical with intense peach and guava flavours.

Coriole Chenin Blanc 2015
McLaren Vale
$12-$19
90/100
Pristine, brightly lit and tangy, with mouthfilling tropical fruits.

Kalleske Florentine Chenin Blanc 2016
Barossa Valley
$12-$19
92/100
Smoky and creamy, with rich peach/melon flavours and soft acids.

Peel Estate Wood-Matured Chenin Blanc 2013
Peel
$30-$49
90/100
Smoky and meaty, with unctuous peach, melon and apricot fruit, cinnamon.

Voyager Estate Chenin Blanc 2015
Margaret River
$12-$19
88/100
Punchy, bright and herbal peach/melon fruit; long and smooth.

Gewürztraminer (or Traminer)

The most spicy and aromatic of all white wine varieties. The best reveal a pungent, floral and rose oil fragrance, which they follow with a luscious, generous palate of lychee-like fruit, some tropical character and musky spices. The finest gewürztraminers typically come from cool climates, where they are able to retain freshness and acidity. Many examples of this variety finish with sweetness to balance out the richness and occasional hardness that can develop.

A variety that originates from Germany and the French region of Alsace, it tends to perform best in Australia from regions like Pipers River (Tasmania), the Adelaide Hills (South Australia) and the Yarra Valley (Victoria). It typically ages quite quickly, and there is a real danger that examples from warmer seasons or warmer climates will become quite oily and broad after just a couple of years in the bottle.

Cassegrain Edition Noir Gewürztraminer 2015

Orange, Hunter Valley

$20-$29

89/100

Pungent and spicy, mineral and savoury, with intense fruit.

Delatite Dead Man's Hill Gewürztraminer 2015

Upper Goulburn

$20-$29

94/100

Musky scents of lychees and rosewater; long, fresh and nervy.

Ros Ritchie Dead Man's Hill Vineyard Gewürztraminer 2014

Mansfield

$20-$29

92/100

Wild, deeply perfumed, musky and meaty, with a lingering savoury, mineral finish.

Skillogalee Gewürztraminer 2014

Clare Valley

$20-$29

91/100

Long, generous and spicy, with musk stick aromas and lychee flavours.

Spring Vale Gewürztraminer 2015

East Coast

$20-$29

91/100

Vibrant, musky and flora, with a long palate of stonefruit and lychees.

Marsanne & Roussanne

THE WHITE VARIETIES

The northern Rhône white varieties of marsanne and Roussanne were introduced to the Yarra Valley (Victoria) more than a century ago. They are now grown throughout central Victoria and in a sprinkling of other regions such as the Barossa Valley (South Australia), Margaret River (Western Australia) and Griffith (New South Wales).

Marsanne originated as the backbone of the white wines of Hermitage and Crozes-Hermitage. Its freshness and zest in youth, its tendency to develop herbal, citrus and honeysuckle fragrances and its ability to mature over a medium term into a lingering, firm, toasty, honeyed and savoury white wine with richness and character make it the complete package. It's for people who like their white wine young and old; it has both personality and distinction.

Roussanne is potentially even more interesting, since its fineness and tightness make it a perfect blending partner with marsanne. By itself, roussanne has a characteristic heady fragrance, a spiciness, a leanness and a soft finish with lively mineral acids. Frequently, in Australia as well as the Rhône Valley, these grapes are blended together, creating a fine synergy between marsanne's length on the palate and roussanne's spicy floral perfume.

St Huberts Roussanne 2015

Yarra Valley

$20-$29

95/100

Fragrant, floral and smoky, with a wonderful line of fruit.

Tahbilk Marsanne 2015

Nagambie Lakes

$12-$19

91/100

Luscious and textured, with honeysuckle aromas and a lemony finish.

Torbreck Marsanne 2015

Barossa Valley

$30-$49

93/100

Long, gentle, smooth and nougat-like.

Yalumba Eden Valley Roussanne 2015

Eden Valley

$20-$29

90/100

Pristine, spicy and waxy, with a luscious core of stonefruit flavour.

Yeringberg Marsanne Roussanne 2015

Yarra Valley

$50-$99

95/100

Creamy, nutty, savoury and earthy; musky and deeply flavoured.

Pinot Gris/ Pinot Grigio

Two of the most popular wines in Australia today are actually made from the same grape variety. There are two different European models for the wines we know as pinot gris and pinot grigio. A pink/grey mutation of pinot noir, pinot gris is a French variety best known for the wines it produces in Alsace, where it's actually called 'Tokay d'Alsace'. As pinot grigio, it is also quite widely planted in the northern Italian regions of Lombardy, Alto Adige and Friuli-Venezia Giulia.

Wines labelled as 'Pinot Gris' are typically rich and floral with mouthfilling pear, peach and apricot flavours and a musky rose oil scent. They can be quite dry or marginally

Coldstream Hills Deer Farm Vineyard Pinot Gris 2015

Yarra Valley

$20-$29

91/100

Floral, long and gentle, delightful pear, apple and peach flavours.

Curly Flat Pinot Gris 2015

Macedon Ranges

$20-$29

91/100

Waxy, spicy, round and mouthfilling, with a refreshing lemony finish.

Holly's Garden Pinot Gris 2015

Whitlands

$20-$29

92/100

Pristine, floral and spicy; juicy and marginally sweet.

Holm Oak Pinot Gris 2015

Tamar Valley

$20-$29

91/100

Vivacious and marginally sweet, with musky spices.

Kilikanoon Skilly Valley Pinot Gris 2015

Clare Valley

$20-$29

93/100

Very floral, generous and juicy; with style shape and a lemony finish.

sweet – either is valid. Harvested earlier, the wines labeled as 'Pinot Grigio' are leaner and drier, with a less opulent but more nutty and citrusy bouquet. They also tend to drink better while young, while their tight, sometimes chalky textures and nutty, citrusy flavours finish savoury, with bone-dry mineral acids.

While many Australian regions make these wines the best pinot gris come from Tasmania, the Adelaide Hills and the Clare Valley (both South Australia), while the better pinot grigio styles are made in the King Valley, Mornington Peninsula (both Victoria) and McLaren Vale (South Australia).

Kooyong Beurrot Pinot Gris 2015

Mornington Peninsula

$30-$49

93/100

Musky, spicy and meaty, with white Turkish delight flavour.

Moorilla Muse Series St Matthias Vineyard Pinot Gris 2015

Tamar Valley

$30-$49

94/100

Laced with violets, lavender and apple blossom; juicy and marginally

Pike & Joyce Pinot Gris 2015

Adelaide Hills

$20-$29

91/100

Floral and faintly herbal, long and chalky. Faintly sweet.

Primo Estate Joseph d'Elena Pinot Grigio 2016

Adelaide

$20-$29

91/100

Frisky and floral, pristine and spicy, with generous flavours.

Tim Adams Pinot Gris 2016

Clare Valley

$20-$29

92/100

Fresh and racy, laced with apple, pear and rose water.

Riesling

Riesling is the principal grape variety behind the famous German wines from the Rhine and Mosel Rivers. While most European wines made from this grape are slightly, moderately or very sweet, the Australian tradition with riesling is to create a long, taut and bone-dry wine without any sugar whatsoever. There is now, however, an emergent class of European-styled rieslings carrying a few grams per litre of residual sugar.

If you're looking for white wines to cellar, it's hard to go past riesling. That said, it can be incredibly bright and vivacious during the first eighteen months of its life. Deeply scented with fresh flowers, citrus blossom and musk, it is often vibrant, long and

Best's Great Western Riesling 2015

Grampians Great Western

$20-$29

95/100

Deeply floral and alluring, long and faintly sweet, superbly refreshing.

Castle Rock Estate Porongorup Riesling 2016

Porongorup

$20-$29

95/100

Profoundly scented and pure; very long, racy and limey.

Henschke Peggy's Hill Riesling 2015

Eden Valley

$20-$29

95/100

Lustrous and refreshing, with pure lime/lemon flavour.

Helm Tumbarumba Riesling 2015

Tumbarumba

$20-$29

94/100

Scented with lemon blossom; long and chalky with juicy flavour.

La Boheme Act One Riesling 2015

Yarra Valley

$12-$19

90/100

Laced with rose oil and lychee, long, mouthfilling and marginally sweet.

racy. Rieslings from the Clare and Eden Valley regions of South Australia are typically laced with scents and tastes of lime juice and lemon. It can also reflect green apples and pears, especially if from the cooler and more southerly regions.

Until it's around five years of age, however, riesling will usually undergo a dull, lacklustre phase while it doesn't have much to say. Then, with bottle-age, riesling develops more richness and palate weight, with the typical development of honeyed, toasty, waxy and oily characters.

As you also find in Germany, a small number of very sweet late-picked dessert wines are made in Australia from riesling, often with the Botrytis cinerea fungus, or 'noble rot' which helps to concentrate flavours.

Australian riesling grows well in a number of regions, but most especially in the Clare Valley and Eden Valley (both South Australia) and in the Great Southern (Western Australia). Clare rieslings are powerfully fruited, dry and citrusy, while those from Eden Valley are typically more chalky and mineral. The finest from the Great Southern are often more flowery and musky, sometimes with suggestions of of guava and green tea. They typically finish with tightly focused acids and suggestions of minerals.

Mitchell Watervale Riesling 2015
Clare Valley
$20-$29
94/100
Tightly focused, with citrusy fruit and a fine chalkiness.

Orlando St Helga Riesling 2015
Eden Valley
$20-$29
96/100
Translucently bright and fresh, deeply floral, long and shapely.

Pikes The Merle Riesling 2015
Clare Valley
$30-$49
96/100
Very long, racy and floral, with a slatey texture.

Seppelt Drumborg Vineyard Riesling 2015
Henty
$30-$49
96/100
Taut and textural, with pristine floral scents; faintly

Tahbilk Riesling 2015
Nagambie Lakes
$12-$19
90/100
Fragrant and lemony, with lively fruit and mouthwatering acids.

Sauvignon Blanc & blends with Semillon

The trendiest white grape around the wine world today, sauvignon blanc is also extremely popular in Australia. The cool Adelaide Hills region (South Australia) makes much of Australia's finest sauvignon blanc, while other fine examples can come from Coonawarra (South Australia), Pemberton, the Great Southern (both Western Australia) and southern Victoria. This grape variety has something of a split personality, since it appears equally capable of presenting fruit-like as well as

   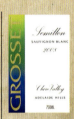

Bay of Fires Sauvignon Blanc 2015
Tasmania
$30-$49
95/100
Pungent, briny and faintly herbal, with vivacious passionfruit flavour.

Cannibal Creek Sauvignon Blanc 2015
West Gippsland
$20-$29
94/100
Punchy and generous, round and luscious, finishing bright and lemony.

Castle Rock Estate Porongorup Sauvignon Blanc 2016
Porongorup
$20-$29
91/100
Laced witih gooseberries and passionfruit, finishing fresh and focused.

Flametree Sauvignon Blanc Semillon 2016
Margaret River
$20-$29
91/100
Lightly herbal, packed with flavour, finishes

Grosset Semillon Sauvignon Blanc 2016
Clare Valley, Adelaide Hills
$30-$49
93/100
Long and chalky, with guava and lychee flavours, frisky acids.

vegetative characters. Its fruit flavours most often resemble passionfruit, gooseberries, lychees and occasionally blackcurrant, while its vegetal spectrum ranges between a light smell of freshly cut grass to capsicum and even asparagus.

Sauvignon blanc performs at its best in cooler climates. Because most Australian vineyards are however located in warmer climate regions, most Australian sauvignon blanc is blended with semillon, increasing its length of flavour on the palate as well as the freshness and raciness of its finish.

They're made and taste quite different to most sauvignon blancs and blends with semillon, but there is an upper crust of less herbaceous, less fruit-driven and quite significantly barrel-aged (and often barrel-fermented) sauvignon blancs and blends, the finest of which are able to cellar for significantly longer than the majority made and sold for immediate to early enjoyment. These are made in a style inspired by the white wines of the Bordeaux region on the west coast of France.

Just like the finest sauvignon blancs of the Loire Valley in France (another of the French regions where the grape originates), the best Australian examples also present some of the chalky textures and mineral finish that enable them to partner food so well.

Peccavi Sauvignon Blanc Semillon 2014

Margaret River

$30-$49

95/100

Wonderful fruit and smoky vanilla oak, long and briny.

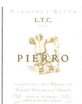

Pierro LTC Semillon Sauvignon Blanc Blend 2015

Margaret River

$30-$49

94/100

Nutty and herbal; long, smooth and

Port Phillip Estate Sauvignon 2015

Mornington Peninsula

$20-$29

93/100

Complex and smoky, generous and savoury, with a briny finish.

SC Pannell Sauvignon Blanc 2015

Adelaide Hills

$20-$29

92/100

Faintly herbal, with a long, seamless presence of punchy fruit.

Shaw and Smith Sauvignon Blanc 2016

Adelaide Hills

$20-$29

93/100

Pristine, spotless and vibrant; stylish and beautifully

Semillon

Another white French variety (from Bordeaux), semillon is suited to either long cellaring or wood maturation to enhance its delicate herbaceous, citrusy and melon-like flavours. Australia's finest region for wines made from 100% semillon is the Hunter Valley (New South Wales). In their youth, they are typically lean, lemony and chalky, but mature Hunter Valley semillons become more fragrant, soft and complex (often quite smoky), with a long, persistent waxy flavour of buttered toast, honey and spice. Traditionally made without oak, they can live for decades.

The Clare Valley (South Australia) produces a more pungent, juicy and vivacious semillon that with a small measure of oak maturation can develop superbly with time in the bottle. The Barossa Valley (also South Australia) typically makes a more

Allandale Semillon 2015
Lower Hunter Valley
$12-$19
91/100
Fresh, dusty and chalky with a citrusy core of lemon and lime juice..

Brokenwood Semillon 2015
Lower Hunter Valley
$20-$29
90/100
Taut and lemony, with a tangy, pithy texture.

Calabria 3 Bridges Botrytis Semillon 2013
Riverina
$20-$29
94/100
Luscious and concentrated, with a sweet core of stonefruit and brulée.

Cassegrain Edition Noir Semillon 2016
Hastings River
$12-$19
91/100
Mouthfilling and chalky, with lingering lime, lemon and melon flavour.

Kilikanoon Pearce Road
Clare Valley
$20-$29
94/100
Smoky melon, vanilla oak and nettle-like notes, long and fresh.

THE WHITE VARIETIES

plush, creamy and generous wine that can be given some maturation in oak casks.

Semillon's length on the palate and its racy, refreshing acidity enable it to add to the length of flavour and the complexity of sauvignon blanc, the variety with which it is traditionally blended in France's Bordeaux region. This is today a popular blend in Western Australia, most notably in Margaret River, which could stake a claim to ownership of the Australian style of Semillon Sauvignon Blanc.

Semillon is also one of the few white varieties able to make full, luscious sweet dessert wines with the fungus botrytis cinerea, or noble rot. In Australia, the Riverina region of New South Wales has become the epicentre of this style, using the humidity from the regions' irrigation channels to help develop the fungus that is so essential to this style.

McGuigan The Shortlist Semillon 2015

Lower Hunter Valley

$20-$29

/100

Fragrant and herbal, with light melon and guava flavour.

Mount Horrocks Semillon 2015

Clare Valley

$20-$29

94/100

Vivacous fruit knits tightly with creamy, toasty and vanilla oak.

Mount Pleasant Elizabeth Semillon 2015

Lower Hunter Valley

$12-$19

91/100

Bright melon, apple and lime flavours are wrapped in lemony acids.

Thomas Braemore Semillon 2015

Lower Hunter Valley

$20-$29

92/100

Taut and stylish, deeply scented, bright and mineral.

Tyrrell's Vat 1 Semillon 2011

Lower Hunter Valley

$50-$99

93/100

Remarkably fresh and youthful, with a dusty length of lemon juice and melon flavour.

Verdelho

A white wine variety from Portugal, Spain and Madeira that was initially brought to Australia to make fortified wine, verdelho is enjoying a second life as white wine variety suited to dry or slightly off-dry table wine. Typically, in Australia it makes a medium-bodied but full-flavoured wine with a juicy, round and generous palate. It's quite herbal and spicy, with a vibrant spectrum of gooseberry, guava and peachy flavour in its youth than can finish with a fresh flinty aspect. After just a few years it becomes quite rich and honeyed – even the finer and more vibrant expressions are likely to become quite luscious and glycerol-like.

While the variety has enjoyed a historic connection with the Hunter Valley (New South Wales), these days Australia's verdelhos tend to come from warmish regions such as several from Western Australia, plus Langhorne Creek and McLaren Vale (both South Australia).

Bremerton Verdelho 2015

Langhorne Creek

$12-$19

87/100

Faintly herbal, long and lean, with lemony acidity and a hint of mineral.

Chapel Hill Verdelho 2015

McLaren Vale

$12-$19

89/100

Punchy and juicy, with some herbal notes and a soft finish.

Fox Creek Verdelho 2015

McLaren Vale

$12-$19

89/100

Smooth and savoury, with spicy aspects and a core of citrusy fruit.

Moondah Brook Verdelho 2015

Western Australia

$12-$19

87/100

Smoky, tobaccoey and herbal, with fresh peachy fruit.

Sandalford Estate Reserve Verdelho 2016

Margaret River

$20-$29

89/100

Brightly lit, juicy and generous, with a rich soft palate of tropical flavour.

Viognier

A scarce variety from Condrieu and Château Grillet in the northern Rhône Valley, viognier is today closely associated with the Eden Valley and Adelaide Hills regions in South Australia, and shows great potential around Geelong (Victoria) and Canberra (ACT).

Viognier has a sumptuous, round texture and an exotic perfume of apricots and citrus blossom with a typical spicy, lingering finish and soft acids. It has more texture and structure than most white varieties. It fits neatly into either serious or alfresco dining, although it is best enjoyed before excessive bottle-age because it can simply become too broad and flabby to really enjoy. It is becoming closely associated with the Eden Valley and Adelaide Hills regions in South Australia, and shows great potential around Geelong (Victoria) and Canberra (ACT).

Viognier is also used in several Australian wine regions to blend in small volumes with shiraz, replicating the classic shiraz viognier blend of Côte-Rôtie in the Rhône Valley, France. When blended with shiraz it contributes spice and perfume to the bouquet, and actually lends firmness and depth to its structure.

Clonakilla Viognier 2015
Canberra
$30-$49
92/100
Scented with spice and honeysuckle, with a savoury palate of melon and apricot.

Millbrook Estate Viognier 2015
Perth Hills
$30-$49
89/100
Floral and spicy, with rich stonefruit flavours.

Torbreck Viognier 2015
Barossa Valley
$30-$49
92/100
Luscious and juicy; deeply fruited, savoury and smoky.

Yalumba Eden Valley Viognier 2015
Eden Valley
$20-$29
92/100
Pristine and floral, long and vibrant with a refreshing lemony finish.

Yeringberg Viognier 2015
Yarra Valley
$30-$49
94/100
Laced with tangerine and lemon blossom, translucently pure and

THE RED VARIETIES

Barbera

Barbera is a spicy and frequently peppery red variety from the Piedmont region in Italy's northeast, where it makes approachable medium-weight but deeply flavoured wines that occasionally reveal an unusual diesel oil/nicotine character. In Australia, barbera makes easy-drinking, fruit-dominant wines with pleasing sour-edged cherry/berry flavours, fine, drying tannins and a typically bright acidity that can even border on tartness.

It's still too early for us to know the definitive best regions for barbera, but the King Valley (Victoria), Hunter Valley (New South Wales) and McLaren Vale (South Australia) are currently at the head of the field.

Coriole Barbera 2014

McLaren Vale

$20-$29

89/100

Searingly intense cherry/plum fruit, dusty tannins and fresh acids.

Dal Zotto Barbera 2014

King Valley

$20-$29

85/100

Spicy and savoury, with flavours of small red berries, plums and cola.

Margan Breaking Ground Barbera 2014

Lower Hunter Valley

$20-$29

90/100

Pungent and jammy; laced with black, blue and red fruits.

Sevenhill Inigo Barbera 2014

Clare Valley

$20-$29

91/100

Earthy and spicy, with intense black and blue fruit flavours.

dell'Uva Barbera 2012

Barossa Valley

$20-$29

92/100

Rustic and fiery; dark fruits and chocolate backed by leather and nicotene.

THE RED VARIETIES

Cabernet Sauvignon & Blends

Cabernet sauvignon is the backbone of the classic reds of the Medoc region on the left hand side of the estuary and river system in Bordeaux, France. Indeed, it is found in some proportion in all but a small percentage of all Bordeaux red wines, often blended with its close relative, cabernet franc, or its more distant relations of merlot, malbec and petit verdot. It is also grown in most Australian wine regions.

It's perhaps unfair, but cabernet sauvignon is anything but everyone's pin-up red wine these days. Because it takes so long to develop complexity and intrigue it can look a little dull and uninteresting while young, especially next to some of the wilder, more spicy, fragrant and meaty pinot noir, shiraz and shiraz blends that tend to dominate wine lists in hip restaurants and cafes.

Bowen Estate Cabernet Sauvignon 2014
Coonawarra
$30-$49
96/100
Classically firm and textured, perfect dark berry fruit and fine oak.

Deep Woods Estate Reserve Cabernet Sauvignon 2014
Margaret River
$50-$99
95/100
Elegant and silky, supple and deeply perfumed. Stylish.

Dominique Portet Yarra Valley Cabernet Sauvignon 2014
Yarra Valley
$30-$49
93/100
Sumptuous, firm and structured, with dense plum/cassis fruit.

Hardys Nottage Hill Cabernet Shiraz 2015
South Eastern Australia
$5-$11
87/100
Brightly lit, smooth and polished, with vibrant sweet berry fruit

Lake Breeze Cabernet Sauvignon 2014
Langhorne Creek
$20-$29
91/100
Firm and structured, with a deep core of minty blackcurrant flavour.

continued
Cabernet Sauvignon & Blends

Young cabernet sauvignon is scented with violets, blackberries, mulberries and dried herbs. It's firm, drying and astringent, with deep flavours of small black and red berries, perhaps also of mint, mineral and dark chocolate. It might be slightly 'hollow' in the middle of the palate – a deficiency that winemakers typically resolve by blending with it such varieties as merlot, or even shiraz that provide depth and richness to the mid palate.

Of all the popular grape varieties, cabernet sauvignon is perhaps definitively the most ordered and structured in its youth. It needs to be this way to deliver the classic qualities expected of great cabernet with great age.

As cabernet sauvignon matures, it steadily evolves cedary, cigarboxy and even truffle-like complexity, and gradually becomes more smooth and approachable. The finest cabernet sauvignon-based wines from fine vintages are capable of living and developing for at least four to five decades.

The three leading Australian regions for this variety are Margaret River (Western Australia), Coonawarra (South Australia) and the Yarra Valley (Victoria), each of which can produce world-class cabernet for the long haul in the

PETIT VERDOT

The fifth and by far the most minor of the Bordeaux red varieties, petit verdot can make a spicy, highly aromatic wine of startlingly bright and intense red and black berry fruits and an elegant, supple palate. Petit verdot is often at its best while very young, since it tends to lack both the length on the palate and the longevity of varieties like cabernet sauvignon. Most of the time it's blended into red wines with members of its related family, being cabernet sauvignon, merlot, cabernet franc and malbec.

Try Millbrook's Petit Verdot (Perth Hills) or Pirramimma's juicy release (McLaren Vale).

CABERNET FRANC

Cabernet franc shares many of the characteristics of its cousin, cabernet sauvignon, but typically needs the support of other varieties in a blend. Like cabernet sauvignon, it's from the French region of Bordeaux where it has most success in blends with merlot on the right hand side of the region's famous river and estuary system.

Australia is hardly awash with examples of 100% cabernet franc but those that perform best are typically from the better cabernet sauvignon regions, but especially the Margaret River region of Western Australia.

Cabernet franc is often blended to cabernet sauvignon and merlot, where its small red berry flavours, slightly herbal aspect, silky tannins and restrained spiciness contribute elements of complexity and structure.

Fine wines from cabernet franc are made by Woodlands (Margaret River) and Redbank Winery (Pyrenees).

THE RED VARIETIES

Primo Estate Zamberlan Cabernet Sauvignon Sangiovese 2015

McLaren Vale

$30-$49

92/100

Sour-edged cassis/cherry fruit and chocolatey oak.

Redman Cabernet Sauvignon 2014

Coonawarra

$20-$29

95/100

Deeply floral, with pristine dark berry/plum fruit and gravelly tannins.

Thorn Clarke Sandpiper Cabernet Sauvignon 2014

Barossa

$12-$19

90/100

Pristine and juicy, generous and smooth.

Woodlands Cabernet Merlot 2014

Margaret River

$20-$29

92/100

Firmish and mineral, with a dusty, herbal presence of cassis and dark plums.

Wynns Coonawarra Estate Black Label Cabernet Sauvignon 2014

Coonawarra

$30-$49

95/100

Long, assertive, deeply flavoured and complete: classic cabernet.

Grenache Blends

Grenache is one of the most important red varieties of the southern Rhône Valley in France, where it is an essential component of many wonderful regional blends, especially with shiraz and mourvèdre. It's also huge in Spain where it's known as garnacha. In Australia, grenache is also a very important variety, since in regions like the Barossa Valley and McLaren Vale (both South Australia), there are vineyards whose century-plus old grenache vines are still producing exceptional wine.

While young, grenache wines have almost a red-blue colour. Often profoundly floral, they are often steeped in wild, brambly and sometimes confectionary flavours of black, red and blue fruits, and can be very meaty and rustic. Grenache does not have a thick skin, so many grenaches can be relatively light in colour. As it ages, grenache typically

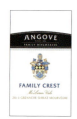

Angove Family Crest Grenache Shiraz Mourvèdre 2015
McLaren Vale
$20-$29
90/100
Generous, juicy flavours of black, blue and red berries; fresh and vibrant.

Glaetzer Wallace Shiraz Grenache 2014
Barossa Valley
$20-$29
90/100
Smooth and polished, with luscious, spicy fruit.

Henschke Johann's Garden Grenache Blend 2015
Barossa Valley
$30-$49
92/100
Heady and floral, with smooth, generous cherry/plum flavour.

Kilikanoon Killerman's Run Shiraz Grenache 2014
Clare Valley
$12-$19
90/100
Spicy, firm and savoury; with lingering dark fruit and menthol.

Morris GSM Grenache Shiraz Mourvedre 201
Rutherglen
$20-$29
93/100
Vibrant, spicy and musky, with briary fruit and fine bony tannins.

THE RED VARIETIES

becomes very meaty and gamey. It's rarely powerful and astringent; rather more smooth, tight-grained and voluptuous.

Grenache is also suited to making fresh, grapey and often savoury rosé styles, which it does quite commonly in France and now quite frequently in Australia.

Here's an odd point: it would be impossible to say truthfully that grenache is a must-have wine for most wine drinkers. Yet when large companies undertake consumer research on the grape whose taste most frequently pleases most wine consumers the answer is nearly always the same: grenache.

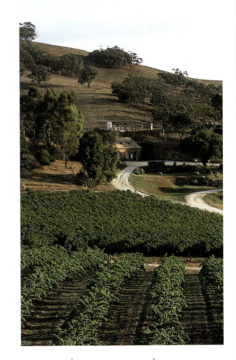

Penfolds Bin 138 Grenache Shiraz Mourvèdre Blend 2014

Barossa Valley

$30-$49

91/100

Peppery, floral and spicy; long, vibrant and fine-grained.

Rosemount Estate GSM Grenache Shiraz Mourvèdre 2014

McLaren Vale

$30-$49

91/100

Spicy berry/plum fruit; long, smooth and polished.

Schwarz Meta Grenache 2014

Barossa Valley

$20-$29

93/100

Fiery, earthy, soft and smooth, with lingering pastille-like fruit.

SC Pannell Grenache 2014

McLaren Vale

$50-$99

91/100

Dusty, peppery; smooth, polished and faintly jammy.

Teusner Joshua Grenache Mataro Shiraz 2015

Barossa Valley

$30-$49

91/100

Musky and jammy; soft, smooth and medium weight.

Malbec

Malbec is another of the five major Bordeaux red varieties although these days it's more popularly associated with Argentina, where it has made a real home and whose wines are significantly different to those of its country of origin.

Warmer-climate malbec can be deep firm and fiery – just the sort of thing to handle a South American barbecue. Yet from cooler climates and if made with a more Francophilic philosophy, it can be delicate, perfumed and fine-grained. Its principal role in Bordeaux is to fill out the palate of and give more firmness to cabernet and merlot-based wines.

Most Australian examples are firmer and more generous, with a rich middle palate, loads of colour but not necessarily a great deal of finesse. In Australia, it is planted in small patches, generally in premium wine areas such as the Clare Valley (South Australia), Frankland River and Margaret River (both Western Australia), where our finest malbec is made. In South Australia's Langhorne Creek, makers are now showing it renewed respect, producing fuller-flavoured wines of richness and depth. Less distinguished in character than cabernet sauvignon or merlot, it occasionally has a greenish aspect in its youth that resembles boiled vegetables.

Bleasdale Generations Malbec 2014
Langhorne Creek
$30-$49
94/100
Handsomely oaked; deep, dark, firmish and expressive.

Brothers in Arms Side by Side Malbec 2014
Langhorne Creek
$30-$49
90/100
Wild, floral and meaty, with a long palate of fiery fruit and refreshing

Deep Woods Estate Malbec 2014
Margaret River
$20-$29
90/100
Vibrant and elegant, with pristine cherry/plum flavour and fresh oak.

Ferngrove King Malbec 2014
Frankland River
$20-$29
91/100
Fragant, sweetly oaked, long and pastille-like.

Wendouree Malbec 2013
Clare Valley
$50-$99
95/100
Searingly intense but polished, perfumed and velvety.

Merlot

THE RED VARIETIES

Merlot is the second most important red variety from Bordeaux although it's more widely planted there than cabernet sauvignon. An earlier-ripening grape than cabernet sauvignon, merlot is able to produce a fuller spectrum of flavour in cooler seasons than cabernet sauvignon. It also has a more profound presence in the middle of the palate (where cabernet sauvignon may be lacking, especially in cooler seasons) – the historic reason why it is blended so often with cabernet sauvignon. Merlot's ripe flavours of dark cherries, plums and earthy, meaty and fruitcake-like undertones are also very compatible with the flavours of cabernet.

Not surprisingly, most of the better merlot grown in Australia is actually blended with cabernet sauvignon. If it is made as a 100% varietal wine, Australian merlot is typically soft and fleshy, and is frequently early to mature. The finest straight merlots come from Coonawarra (South Australia), the Yarra Valley (Victoria) and Margaret River (Western Australia).

A winemaking secret is that a small percentage of cabernet sauvignon can give a little more length and structure to merlot's palate. Another secret is that Australia has not had much high-quality merlot planting material to play with – until now. This breed is about to get a whole lot better!

Giant Steps Sexton Vineyard Merlot 2014

Yarra Valley

$30-$49

95/100

Classic cherry/plum varietal qualities with meaty undertones. Smooth.

Jacob's Creek Classic Merlot 2015

South Eastern Australia

$5-$11

87/100

Smooth and juicy with charming sweet fruit and soft tannins.

Leconfield Merlot 2014

Coonawarra

$20-$29

91/100

Minty, dark-fruited, smooth and pliant.

Parker Coonawarra Estate Terra Rossa Merlot 2014

Coonawarra

$30-$49

93/100

Polished, smooth and chocolatey, with lingering sour-edged fruits.

Primo Estate Merlesco Merlot 2016

McLaren Vale

$12-$19

89/100

Earthy, dark and meaty; very approachable and ready to

Nebbiolo

Nebbiolo is one of Italy's principal quality red grapes whose plantings are centred on Piedmont, but also in Lombardy and the Valle d'Aosta. The classic wines of nebbiolo, sold as Barolo and Barbaresco, are robust, taught and firm, with more depth and structure than the prettier and more fruit-focused nebbiolos from the surrounding Lange area within Piedmont.

Nebbiolo's heady floral and earthy perfumes and typical flavours of cherries, raspberries, truffles, tobacco and burnt asphalt. They share qualities of perfume, structure and a translucency with pinot noir, so it's unsurprising that if you become a devotee of one of these varieties, chances are that you'll love the other. Occasionally quite tannic, nebbiolo can reveal a firm, drying astringency, and can take decades to reach full maturity.

Nebbiolo is a newcomer to Australia, with the best wines to date coming from Heathcote, the King Valley (both Victoria), Hilltops (New South Wales), Adelaide Hills and McLaren Vale (both South Australia).

Giaconda Nebbiolo 2012

Beechworth

$50-$99

95/100

Classically perfumed, fine-grained, long and savoury.

Grove Estate Sommita Nebbiolo 2015

Hilltops

$30-$49

94/100

Deeply floral; long, juicy and chocolatey.

Jasper Hill Georgia's Paddock Nebbiolo 2014

Heathcote

$50-$99

94/100

Wild and brambly, with a long, firm and sour-edged palate.

Mountainside Nebbiolo 2015

Grampians

$20-$29

92/100

Perfumed and earthy, with intense blood plum and citrus flavour.

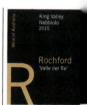

Rochford King Valley Nebbiolo 2015

King Valley

$30-$49

93/100

Medium to full-bodied, lightly funky, long and savoury

Pinot Noir

THE RED VARIETIES

Pinot noir is the illustrious red variety of Burgundy. Of all red grapes, this is the hardest, to grow and to make and whose wine is possibly the hardest to follow from a standing start. But don't be frightened – it's worth all the trouble! The classic cliché with pinot is 'the iron fist in the velvet glove', which reflects its legendary ability to deliver some of the most heady perfumes and most intense flavours that any wine can offer, but in a mode of sheer finesse and seduction.

Originating in a cool climate, pinot noir performs its best in the cooler Australian regions of the Yarra Valley, Mornington Peninsula, Geelong, Gippsland and Macedon Ranges (all Victoria) as well as the Coal River Valley, East Coast and Tamar Valley regions of the southernmost state, Tasmania. The Adelaide Hills (South Australia) and the Great Southern (Western Australia) can also make convincing pinot noir.

Young pinot noir has a comparatively translucent colour, but don't be too bothered over this. Unlike most other red wines, pinot noir can also appear to be excessively mature and developed from the perspective of colour, yet can still be at its very peak. The finest young pinots reveal a heady, alluring perfume of rose petals, cherries and dark berries, while their palates can deliver a surprising depth and intensity of powerful flavour despite a restraint and elegance that can border or ethereal and fragile. As they age, pinot noir moves into an entirely different spectrum of flavour, since it

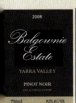

Balgownie Estate Yarra Valley Pinot Noir 2015
Yarra Valley
$20-$29
90/100
Smooth, pristine and perfumed, with fresh cherry/berry flavour.

Bindi Original Vineyard Pinot Noir 2015
Macedon Ranges
$50-$99
95/100
Profoundly musky, floral and fine-grained.

Dalrymple Cottage Block Pinot Noir 2014
Pipers River
$30-$49
92/100
Smoky and floral, with pristine fruit and a soft

De Bortoli Yarra Valley Estate Grown Pinot Noir 2015
Yarra Valley
$30-$49
93/100
Spicy, smoky and faintly meaty; fine and elegant.

Freycinet Louis Pinot Noir 2015
East Coast Tasmania
$30-$49
93/100
Pristine, intense and mouthfilling, builds towards the finish.

continued
Pinot Noir

can become rather meaty and gamey. The wines become more savoury and delicate as they mature, but can retain unexpected vitality of flavour and vibrancy of acidity.

Perhaps more than just about any other red grape variety, pinot noir provides an extremely precise reflection of its site and vintage. Minor changes in soil type, slope or exposure to wind can result in a wine of different identity. If all other things are equal, the difference in wine quality between the great sites and the lesser sites for pinot noir is quite incredible, and is extremely obvious to taste. Around the world, the number of truly great sites for pinot noir is actually quite small, which is why the elite pinot noirs from Burgundy, Australia, New Zealand and Oregon are so expensive and sought after.

Pike & Joyce Pinot Noir 2015
Adelaide Hills
$30-$49
91/100
Brightly lit, floral and fine-grained; likely to build.

Port Phillip Estate Red Hill Pinot Noir 2015
Mornington Peninsula
$30-$49
93/100
Lively cherry/plum fruit backed by toasty oak and underbrush.

St Huberts Pinot Noir 2015
Yarra Valley
$30-$49
91/100
Elegant, pristine and translucently clear, with heady, musky aromas.

Stoney Vineyard Pinot Noir 2015
Coal River Valley
$30-$49
91/100
Deep, luscious and pastille-like, with firmness and length.

Stonier Pinot Noir 2015
Mornington Peninsula
$20-$29
93/100
Scented with rose petals, supple and mouthfilling.

Sangiovese

Sangiovese is the major Tuscan red variety where it is the backbone of Chianti and Brunello di Montalcino. Highly floral and often spicy, with translucent, bright sour-edged plum and cherry-like fruit and a fine-grained astringent backbone, it occasionally reveals tobaccoey, rustic and meaty aspects. It's medium to full in body and its taut, refreshing acidity and drying texture help it to complement traditional Italian cuisine.

A relative newcomer to Australia, its finest wines are presently coming from Heathcote, the King Valley (both Victoria), Mudgee (New South Wales), and McLaren Vale (South Australia). Some growers, such as Pizzini in Victoria's King Valley are experimenting by blending it with some other traditional Tuscan red varieties such as Canaiolo and Colorino. Many Australian vineyards and wineries are still experimenting with sangiovese, so it stands to reason that in a few years time, it might have found new homes in some unexpected wine regions.

Castagna La Chiave Sangiovese 2013
Beechworth
$50-$99
96/100
Superbly balanced, with layers of translucent

Coriole Sangiovese 2015
McLaren Vale
$20-$29
92/100
Spicy, earthy and fine-grained, with bright cherry, berry and plum flavour.

Fairbank Sangiovese 2015
Bendigo
$20-$29
90/100
Dark-fruited and chocolatey, long and sour-edged.

Pizzini Lana Il Nastro Gallo 2014
King Valley
$20-$29
90/100
Earthy, floral and savoury, lean and vibrant.

Tar & Roses Sangiovese 2015
Heathcote
$20-$29
91/100
Smooth and pristine, with mouthfilling varietal fruit.

Shiraz (or Syrah) & Blends

If there is a single wine associated with Australia today, that wine is certainly shiraz (often called 'syrah'). Australian shiraz has forever altered the way that wines from this grape are grown, made and marketed around the world. More than any other wine, shiraz put Australia on the modern wine map.

Shiraz originated near the northern Rhône Valley in France, where today it remains the backbone of the wines of Hermitage, Crozes-Hermitage and Côte-Rôtie. It has been grown in Australia for nearly two centuries, and Australia remains home to many shiraz vineyards whose actual producing vines are well in excessive 100 years

Brokenwood Hunter Valley Shiraz 2014

Lower Hunter Valley

$30-$49

94/100

Classic elegant, savoury medium-bodied Hunter shiraz.

Frankland Estate Shiraz 2015

Frankland River

$20-$29

91/100

Medium in weight, perfumed and peppery, with meaty fruit.

Heathcote Estate Single Vineyard Shiraz 2014

Heathcote

$30-$49

94/100

Sumptuous dark fruit, measured oak and firmness.

Houghton The Bandit Frankland River Shiraz 2014

Frankland River

$20-$29

92/100

Dark berries, black pepper and fine, drying tannins.

John Duval Entity Shiraz 2014

Barossa Valley

$30-$49

93/100

Smooth and luscious, with piercing berry/plum flavour.

THE RED VARIETIES

of age. The oldest individual shiraz vineyard still producing an estate wine is Langmeil's ancient The Freedom Vineyard in the Barossa Valley (South Australia), which was planted in the 1847.

Australia's revered and ancient vineyards of top genetic material, which typically still produce healthy, normal-yielding crops for their regions, deliver intense concentration, layers of fruit and flavour, plus a unique velvet-like mouthfeel. They also provide Australia with an unbeatable advantage in terms of vineyard quality that is the envy of the rest of the wine world.

Because Australia is so large a country, and because its wine regions are located in everything from the warmest, driest parts of the country to cooler regions that are occasionally covered by snow in winter, there is a lot more to Australian shiraz than the ripe and juicy popular brands that are so popular around the world.

While the warmer South Australian regions of the Barossa Valley and McLaren Vale are rightly known for the richness, concentration and smoothness of their shiraz, the cooler regions in the country's southeast produce more restrained, savoury and spicy shiraz, which can often reveal intense pepper-like qualities. Warmer regions typically create shiraz whose depth and structure

Oliver's Taranga Shiraz 2014
McLaren Vale
$20-$29
94/100
Brilliant peppery, fuller-bodied McLaren Vale shiraz.

Redman Shiraz 2014
Coonawarra
$20-$29
92/100
Stylish, medium-bodied and floral, with juicy fruit.

Shaw and Smith Shiraz 2014
Adelaide Hills
$30-$49
95/100
Minty, spicy, long and measured; velvety and savoury.

Tintara Shiraz 2014
McLaren Vale
$20-$29
95/100
Very polished, densely packed and searingly intense.

Torbreck The Struie Shiraz 2014
Barossa Valley, Eden Valley
$30-$49
94/100
Musky, spicy, warm and unctuous; ultra-ripe and

continued
Shiraz (or Syrah) & Blends

are based on their sheer weight and concentration of fruit.

Those that ripen later in cooler climates tend to be supported by a finer, but firm grade of tannin. The best examples of these wines, from regions like Grampians Great Western and the Yarra Valley (each Victoria), the Adelaide Hills (South Australia) and the Great Southern (Western Australia) are long, fine-grained and savoury. They often deliver piercingly intense flavours but remain both restrained and refined.

Warmer inland regions such as Bendigo, Beechworth and Heathcote (Victoria), Mudgee, Hilltops (New South Wales) and the Clare Valley (South Australia) are able to make firm, long-living and profoundly textured shirazes with layers of dense fruit.

While the smell, taste and structure of shiraz does indeed vary from vineyard to vineyard, winemakers have many options when making it. A major decision concerns the type of oak used for its maturation. Following the lead of Australia's most prestigious red wine, Penfolds' Grange, many warmer climate shirazes have been matured in American oak casks, which impart sweet notes of vanilla and coconut ice to the wine. Typically more savoury and cedary, French oak casks provide perhaps a more appropriate alternative. French oak is predominant amongst the more spicy and restrained shirazes from cooler Australian regions and is now being used to craft more elegant and integrated wines from warmer regions.

Tempranillo & Blends

The principal Spanish red variety, tempranillo is most closely associated with the smooth, rustic reds of Rioja and the more powerfully constructed modern wines of the Ribero del Duero. Much of Australia's winegrowing landscape is strikingly similar to the environment in which tempranillo evolved, so it is hardly surprising that it is adapting extremely well to its new home in Australia.

While tempranillo is still a very recent arrival in Australia, it is becoming quite clear that regions such as the Clare Valley, McLaren Vale, the Barossa Valley and Adelaide Hills (all South Australia) as well as Heathcote (Victoria) and are ideally suited to it. At its best, as a dark, brooding red, tempranillo delivers deep flavours of dark plums, dark chocolates, blackberries and polished leather. It can be silky-smooth or rather aggressive and astringent.

Corymbia Dry Red 2014
Swan Valley
$30-$49
93/100
Steeped in vibrant, fiery fruit, long and textured.

Gemtree Luna Roja Tempranillo 2015
McLaren Vale
$20-$29
92/100
Pristine, floral and finely balanced, with juicy, confectionary fruit.

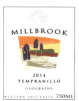

Millbrook Tempranillo 2014
Geographe
$20-$29
92/100
Long and chocolatey, with brightly lit, briary dark fruit.

Running With Bulls Barossa Tempranillo 2015
Barossa
$20-$29
91/100
Wild and smoky; steeped in blackberry, blueberry fruit.

Tar & Roses Tempranillo 2015
Heathcote
$20-$29
90/100
Gentle, bright and juicy, with meaty, tarry undertones.

SPARKLING WINES

It is just thirty years since the arrival of Domaine Chandon in Victoria's Yarra Valley changed the face of Australian sparkling wine. With an emphasis on using the classic Champagne varieties of pinot noir, chardonnay and pinot meunier sourced from this country's cooler regions, plus an approach in both the philosophical and technical areas straight from the heart of Champagne, Domaine Chandon demonstrated, as it continues to do, that Australia can make sparkling wine to rival that from France.

With the subsequent growth of regions like the Adelaide Hills and several across Tasmania – which is today the source of most top-end Australian sparkling wine – the breed has continued to improve. Headed by Accolade's ground-breaking House of Arras brand, a range which

Bay of Fires Tasmanian Cuvée Pinot Noir Chardonnay NV

Tasmania

$30-$49

91/100

Elegant, smooth and crackly, with freshness and focus.

Chandon Vintage Brut 2012

Southern Australia

$30-$49

91/100

Complex and crunchy, long and creamy,

Delamere Vineyards Non–Vintage Rosé NV

Pipers River

$30-$49

91/100

Fragrant and creamy, with fresh cherry, raspberry and strawberry flavour.

Deviation Road Loftia Vintage Brut 2012

Adelaide Hills

$30-$49

93/100

Fresh lemony and red berry/cherry fruit with creamy, nutty complexity.

House of Arras A by Arras Premium Cuvée NV

Tasmania

$20-$29

92/100

Stylish, creamy and medium-bodied, with nutty, honeyed development.

THE SPARKLING WINES

really takes Champagne head-on, the current brood of top-end Australian sparkling wines is arguably the world's finest collection outside France.

Australia is also home to its indigenous sparkling wine – sparkling red. Known for more than its first century as 'Sparkling Burgundy', it is made with the same technique as Champagne, except that the base wine is red instead. It's something people either love or hate – there is no middle ground. The finest examples live for several decades.

House of Arras Brut Elite Sparkling White No. 801
Tasmania
$30-$49
94/100
Long, fragrant and austere, with citrusy fruit and brisk acidity.

Jansz Tasmania Vintage Cuvée Sparkling White 2010
Pipers River
$30-$49
95/100
Developing and buttery, with notes of brioche and bakery yeasts.

Seppelt Original Sparkling Shiraz 2013
Victoria
$12-$19
92/100
Smoky and peppery, meaty and plummy; finishing marginally

Yarrabank Cuvée Sparkling 2011
Victoria
$30-$49
93/100
Mineral and chalky, taut and focused, with elegance and flavour.

Yellowglen Perle Sparkling White 2012
$20-$29
94/100
Fresh stonefruit and citrus flavour; round, gentle and savoury.

ROSÉ

*I*t's taken some time, but Australian winemakers are now taking rosé seriously. Why? Because of consumer demand for the lightness, freshness, taste and structure of quality rosé, plus the undoubted truth that our climate suits its al fresco qualities quite perfectly.

Rosé can be made virtually anywhere. Warmer climates typically produce flavoursome rosés from grenache and shiraz, with just a little more fruit sweetness than the more savoury rosés from pinot noir, cabernet franc, sangiovese and nebbiolo in cooler regions. Certainly, as more grapes of Italian and Spanish origin find their way here, a new breed of more savoury rosé is beginning to emerge.

The best rosés are light, drier and

Angove Nine Vines Rose 2015
South Australia
$12-$19
88/100
Floral and spicy, with fresh cherry flavour and a savoury finish.

Chandon Pinot Noir Rosé 2016
Yarra Valley
$30-$49
89/100
Juicy cherry/berry flavours, hint of citrus, finishes almost dry.

Delamere Vineyards Rosé 2016
Pipers River
$20-$29
90/100
Soft and luscious, with juicy fruit and a savoury, slightly meaty finish.

Fairbank Rosé 2015
Bendigo
$20-$29
90/100
Fresh and restrained, with charming fruit and minerality.

Hardys The Chronicles The Sage Grenache Rosé 2015
Langhorne Creek
$12-$19
87/100
Juicy, confectionary and fragrant; refreshing to finish.

ROSÉ

still, with an attractive pink colour showing no more than the occasional trace of orange. Rosé is essentially informal and uncomplicated, so the best are mainly made without the complexity so sought after in better white or red varietal wines. Their aroma should be vibrant, fresh and fruity, even grapey (?!). Rosé should taste similarly lively and exuberant, with a similar zing of acidity to a riesling. Better examples from pinot noir and sangiovese can finish with a nutty, savoury dryness.

La Boheme Act Two Dry Pinot Noir Rosé 2016
Yarra Valley
$20-$29
87/100
Fragrant and meaty, generous and marginally

Longview Vineyard Nebbiolo Rosato 2016
Adelaide Hills
$20-$29
88/100
Floral and peppery, with candied citrus and raspberry flavour.

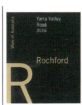

Rochford Yarra Valley Rosé 2016
Yarra Valley
$20-$29
91/100
Charming freshness and flavour, with meaty and savoury undertones.

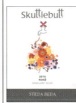

Skuttlebutt Rosé 2016
Margaret River
$12-$19
88/100
Fresh, lively and faintly herbal, with bright cherry/berry fruit.

Vinea Marson Rose 2014
Heathcote
$20-$29
90/100
Savoury and brightly flavoured with cherries, berries and citrusy notes.

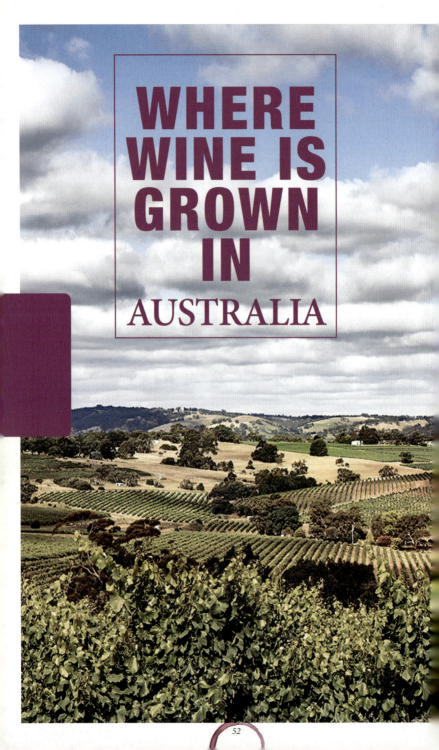

WHERE WINE IS GROWN IN AUSTRALIA

What is a wine region?

Wherever wine is grown, vineyards usually cluster together. The same thing happens in most forms of agriculture, as over time we discover that certain districts are best suited to a particular kind of fruit or crop, or the husbandry of a particular kind of farmed animal.

A number of factors might be the cause of a wine region existing exactly where it does. It might be geological, reflecting in the presence of a particularly favourable soil type such as the terra rossa of regions like Coonawarra (South Australia) or the 100 million year-old degraded greenstone of Heathcote (Victoria). Certain soils, like those of the Eden Valley (South Australia) might imbue their wines with a distinctive chalkiness and minerality.

Climate is another factor that determines the locations and boundaries of wine regions. Some regions exist because they are high enough up a mountain range to be cooler than the comparatively hot districts that surround them, such as Beechworth, high in the hills of northeast Victoria. Aspect and slope are also important in some cases, especially in the example of Burgundy (France), whose most famous segment (the Côte d'Or) would probably fail to make great wine did it not face the directions of east and southeast.

In older times, before mechanised transport, it was also important for wine regions to be close to their markets. Today, the most popular wine regions are usually found within two to three hours' drive from major cities, since they also depend on the constant presence of buyers, visitors and tourists.

Over time, it becomes clear which grape varieties perform best in any given region. Some might even reveal a unique and special synergy that stands their wine apart from that made from the same variety but grown elsewhere. While new and different grape varieties continue to be introduced to Australia with often surprising results, it is today possible to link Australia's best wine regions with a number of grape varieties with which they share in this synergy and association. So here, state by state, is a listing of the most important wine regions in Australia.

WHAT IS NEEDED FOR A COLLECTION OF VINEYARDS TO BECOME A WINE REGION?

To be identified as a single wine region, the area in question must be a single tract of land, comprising at least five independently owned wine grape vineyards of at least 5 ha each. Total production will exceed 500 tonnes of wine grapes a year. A region is required to be measurably discrete from adjoining regions and have measurable homogeneity in grape growing conditions and attributes over its area.

NSW

Australia's first vineyards were planted in New South Wales, the country's most populous state. Today New South Wales is seeing a remarkable period of expansion and discovery, with the recognition of a number of new wine regions.

Canberra

While Australia's capital city, from which this region takes its name, is found in the Australian Capital Territory, a slice of land carved out of New South Wales, most of the vineyards that comprise the Canberra wine region are actually found outside the ACT, in New South Wales – hence its listing here.

With a moderate and mild continental climate that thanks to its altitude makes it operate as more of a cool region, Canberra is capable of a wide array of quality wine from a number of varieties, namely riesling, chardonnay, shiraz, pinot noir and the Rhône Valley white grapes of marsanne and roussanne. Its shiraz is typically savoury, perfumed and medium-bodied, often laced with nuances of cracked pepper. Famously, thanks to the efforts of Clonakilla, Canberra is very much an Australian home of the shiraz viognier blend.

The region is geographically diverse, with a wide range of soils and aspects, so growers have an opportunity to marry site with style. Most wineries are relatively small, so Canberra's output is not large. Its quality enables it to punch far above its weight.

Clonakilla Ballinderry Cabernet Blend 2013
Canberra
$30-$49
92/100
Supple, perfumed and elegant; medium weight and silky.

Clonakilla Shiraz Viognier 2015
Canberra
$100-$199
96/100
Lustrous and perfumed, deeply flavoured, medium-bodied and savoury.

Helm Premium Riesling 2015
Canberra
$30-$49
95/100
Heady and penetrative; pristine floral bouquet, pear and citrus.

Lark Hill Scuro Sangiovese Shiraz 2015
Canberra
$50-$99
93/100
Musky, dark-fruited and floral; elegant and savoury.

The Vintner's Daughter

BEST CANBERRA CELLAR DOORS

NAME	ADDRESS	CONTACT	SPECIAL FACILITIES
Shaw Vineyard Estate	34 Isabel Drive Murrumbateman NSW 2582	(02) 6227 5827 sales@shawvineyards.com.au www.shawvineyards.com.au	Enjoy a modern European meal or wood oven pizza or purchase local jams, olive oils and chocolates. A shearing shed gallery displays work from local artists plus hand painted Italian ceramics.
Clonakilla	3 Crisps Lane, Murrumbateman NSW 2582	(02) 6227 5877 wine@clonakilla.com.au www.clonakilla.com.au	Guests enjoy tasting wine in front of the large fireplace in the new cellar door with views of the surrounding vineyard, including renovated Clonakilla windmill at the top of the hill.
Lerida Estate	87 The Vineyards Collector NSW 2581	(02) 4848 0231 wine@leridaestate.com www.leridaestate.com.au	Visitors can enjoy a stroll through the vineyard, a fly over and view from above in a helicopter or hot air balloon, share a meal or coffee at Café Lerida or participate in a game of Pétanque.
Mount Majura	88 Lime Kiln Road Majura ACT 2609	(02) 6262 3070 info@mountmajura.com.au www.mountmajura.com.au	Guests are offered a complimentary Gumboot Tour, self guided 'nature trail' through the vineyard. Cheese plates and regional tasting plates are also available.

Hilltops

An emerging inland region whose elevation in the hills around the Great Dividing Range of mountains helps to moderate its summer temperatures. Located around the town of Young, it is a relatively cool location whose wines tend to sit between traditional Australian wines from warmer climates and those from established cool regions. Its rainfall is mainly around spring – summer and autumn can be dry indeed.

Hilltops has demonstrated great potential with shiraz, cabernet sauvignon, chardonnay and even the Italian varieties of nebbiolo, rondinella and corvina. Its reds are characteristically perfumed, firm and intense, and offer genuine cellaring potential.

Clonakilla Hilltops Shiraz 2015
Hilltops
$20-$29
91/100
Elegant, fragrant and peppery, with bright red, blue and black fruits.

Freeman Fortuna Pinot Gris Plus 2013
Hilltops
$20-$29
90/100
Wild and meaty, with a nutty, melon-like palate.

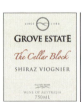

Grove Estate The Cellar Block Shiraz Viognier 2015
Hilltops
$30-$49
94/100
Spotlessly pristine and fragrant; elegant and medium-

McWilliam's Hilltops Shiraz 2013
Hilltops
$20-$29
90/100
Spicy and peppery, leathery and flavoursome.

Moppity Vineyards Reserve Shiraz 2014
Hilltops
$50-$99
93/100
Restrained, minty, briary and herbal; waiting to explode.

JEREMY'S PICK OF HILLTOPS CELLAR DOORS

NAME	ADDRESS	CONTACT	SPECIAL FACILITIES
Freeman	101 Prunevale Road Prunevale NSW 2587	(02) 6384 4299 sales@freemanvineyards.com.au www.freemanvineyards.com.au	Discover the home of Australia's only plantings of two northern Italian grape varieties - Rondinella and Corvina.
Grove Estate	4100 Murringo Road Young NSW 2594	(02) 6382 6999 info@groveestate.com.au www.groveestate.com.au	Enjoy intimate tastings by the cozy fire or on the deck.

Hunter Valley

An historic region to the north and west of Sydney, Australia's largest city. Home to a number of ancient vineyards, especially shiraz, this region exists despite low-yielding soils and a challenging climate. Usually warm and dry (except when grapes are often harvested), the Hunter become home to Australia's most unique white wine, from the semillon variety. Typically harvested early, creating wines with low alcoholic strength and crisp acidity, Hunter semillons can age superbly for significantly more than a decade, developing remarkable complexity as they do. The Hunter also produces elegant, citrusy, melon-like chardonnay that can reveal nuances of

Briar Ridge Stockhausen Shiraz 2014

Lower Hunter Valley

$30-$49

94/100

Sumptously flavoured, peppery and mineral. Long term.

Capercaillie The Ghillie Shiraz 2014

Lower Hunter Valley

$30-$49

92/100

Ripe, wild and fiery, with meaty dark berry flavour.

De Iuliis Limited Release Shiraz 2014

Lower Hunter Valley

$50-$99

93/100

Showy and deeply packed, smooth and sumptuous.

De Iuliis LDR Vineyard Shiraz Touriga 2014

Lower Hunter Valley

$30-$49

91/100

Long, taut and shapely, with pristine fruit and a taut acidity.

Lake's Folly Chardonnay 2015

Lower Hunter Valley

$50-$99

96/100

Classically focused and regional, with intense lemony fruit and acids.

Margan White Label Semillon 2015	Mount Pleasant Mothervine Pinot Noir 2014	Scarborough The Obsessive Chardonnay 2014	Tyrrell's Single Vineyard Stevens Shiraz 2014	Tyrrell's Vat 8 Shiraz Cabernet 2014
Lower Hunter Valley	Lower Hunter Valley	Lower Hunter Valley	Lower Hunter Valley	Lower Hunter Valley
$30-$49	$30-$49	$30-$49	$30-$49	$50-$99
91/100	90/100	92/100	94/100	95/100
Fragrant, long and brittle; with a pithy texture and bright citrusy fruit.	Fine-grained and fairnly meaty; an elegant, savoury Hunter red.	Handsomely oaked, soft and luscious, fragrant and savoury.	Perfumed and musky, elegant and savoury, long and mineral.	Gentle and seamless, pristine and floral, fresh and minty.

continued Hunter valley

tobacco leaf and cumquat which can prove quite cellar-worthy.

Home to an equally distinctive, spicy and savoury expression of shiraz, the Hunter is less successful with most other red varieties, with the possible emerging exception of barbera. Classic Hunter shiraz doesn't need a long, warm season to develop complex, savoury, medium-bodied wines. Sure, the not infrequent wetter seasons produce more herbal, earlier-drinking styles, but the fine years – of which 2014 is a truly stunning example – create wines that live and develop in the bottle for 3-5 decades.

The Hunter Valley is essentially two entirely separate regions – the Upper and Lower Hunter. The Lower Hunter, geographically south of the Upper, roughly consists of the vineyards that have remained around Pokolbin and Rothbury from the boom that lasted until the mid-60's, plus more recent plantings. This is the heart of the region and its most famous names and classic wines are found here.

The Upper Hunter – mainly planted between the Great Dividing range in the west and Musswellbrook in the east, has historically produced larger volumes of simmilar but less distinguished wine.

JEREMY'S PICK OF HUNTER VALLEY CELLAR DOORS

NAME	ADDRESS	CONTACT	SPECIAL FACILITIES
Audrey Wilkinson	750 De Beyers Road Pokolbin NSW 2320	02 4998 7411 cellardoor@audreywilkinson.com.au www.audreywilkinson.com.au	Featuring a cellar door with incredible views, a wine heritage museum and two delightful Vineyard cottages.
	179 Gillards Road Pokolbin NSW 2320	(02) 6382 6999 info@groveestate.com.au www.groveestate.com.au	Enjoy a structured wine tasting at your own private table with complimentary cheese platter.
Tulloch	638 De Beyers Road Pokolbin NSW 2320	(02) 4998 7563 info@scarboroughwine.com.au www.scarboroughwine.com.au	Book bespoke wine and food experiences including Wine & Chocolate, Mystery Wine Tour, Discover & Explore and Wine Flights served in beautifully appointed tasting spaces.
Tyrrell's	1838 Broke Road Pokolbin NSW 2320	(02) 4993 7000 cellardoor@tyrrells.com.au www.tyrrells.com.au	Offering daily wine tours, premium private tastings and the 'Vertical Decadence', incorporating a luxurious helicopter experience by appointment.

Mudgee

Surrounded on three sides by the mountains of the Great Dividing Range, this picturesque but frequently dry region is both a maker of traditional, robust and age-worthy wines from cabernet sauvignon and shiraz as well as being a potential leader with Italian and Spanish red grape varieties. The region's reds are typically quite firm and well structured, with deep, fiery and often earthy fruit. Its chardonnay can be ripe and juicy, with pleasing length and acidity, while its semillon can mature gracefully.

Botobolar Preservative Free Shiraz 2016
Mudgee
$12-$19
86/100
Plush, juicy and forward, with smoothness, pepper and

Logan Ridge of Tears Shiraz 2014
Mudgee
$30-$49
92/100
Spicy, floral and herbal, with a restrained, gravelly presence of dark fruits.

Logan Weemala Tempranillo 2014
Mudgee
$12-$19
90/100
Bony and stony, with dark plums, chocolates and mineral notes.

Montrose Black Shiraz 2014
Mudgee
$30-$49
91/100
Powerful, fiery and assertive, deeply ripened and meaty; big oak.

Robert Oatley Finisterre Chardonnay 2015
Mudgee
$30-$49
90/100
Powerful, fiery and assertive, deeply ripened and meaty; big oak.

JEREMY'S PICK OF MUDGEE CELLAR DOORS

NAME	ADDRESS	CONTACT	SPECIAL FACILITIES
	603 Henry Lawson Drive Mudgee NSW 2850	1300 304 707 cellardoor@bunnamagoowines.com.au www.bunnamagoowines.com.au	Stunning brand new cellar door facility offering tastings in a light filled space surrounded by sweeping lawns and vineyards.
Di Lusso Estate	162 Eurunderee Lane Mudgee NSW 2850	(02) 6373 3125 sales@dilusso.com.au www.dilusso.com.au	Superb vista overlooking the dam, vineyards and distant mountains while enjoying a range of dining options from the Trattoria.
Logan	1320 Castlereagh Highway Apple Tree Flat NSW 2850	02 6373 1333 info@loganwines.com.au www.loganwines.com.au	Take in the sweeping vineyard and bush views from the glass-encased cellar door while tasting wine accompanied by a cheese plate, a great coffee or a freshly baked cake.
Lowe Family Wine Co.	327 Tinja Lane Mudgee NSW 2850	(02) 6372 0800 cellardoor@lowewine.com.au www.lowewine.com.au	Known for its signature winemaker dinners and organic philosophy, wine tasting platters are also available every day.

Riverina

Home to some of Australia's finest late-harvest dessert wines from the semillon variety, the Riverina is a large, dry inland region that depends on irrigation for its existence. It is an engine-room for several of Australia's most successful international brands, and while it has traditionally been associated with less expensive wines, several producers are now seeking and achieving surprising levels of quality. Its shiraz and cabernet can be rich and flavoursome, while the variety of durif (petit syrah) shows considerable potential. Its Italian cultural heritage is now being expressed with some great value wines from Italian varieties.

Calabria 3 Bridges Durif 2014
Riverina
$20-$29
92/100
Stacked with dark fruit; dense, wild and smoky. Firm and balanced.

Calabria Private Bin Pinot Bianco 2015
Riverina
$12-$19
90/100
Spicy and floral, long and juicy, generous and refreshing.

De Bortoli Noble One Botrytis Semillon 2014
Riverina
$30-$49
92/100
Profoundly sweet and unctuous, with deep, honeyed creme caramele flavour.

Deen de Bortoli Vat Series No 8 Shiraz 2014
Riverina
$5-$11
86/100
Pastille-like black and red berries, smoky vanilla oak, fresh and polished.

Gramp's Botrytis Semillon 201 (375ml)
Riverina
$12-$19
94/100
Sweet but not excessively so; honeyed, luscious and brulée-like.

JEREMY'S PICK OF RIVERINA CELLAR DOORS

NAME	ADDRESS	CONTACT	SPECIAL FACILITIES
Calabria	1283 Brayne Road Griffith NSW 2680	(02) 6969 0800 info@calabriawines.com.au www.calabriawines.com.au	Strong family traditions prevail in this Tuscan inspired cellar door where groups can enjoy cheese platters and winery tours.
De Bortoli	De Bortoli Road Bilbul NSW 2680	(02) 6966 0100 feedback@debortoli.com.au www.debortoli.com.au	Offering superb Italian hospitality, guests are encouraged to bring a picnic to enjoy in the beautiful winery gardens while children are entertained in the playground.
McWilliam's Hanwood Cellar Door	Jack McWilliam Road Hanwood NSW 2190	(02) 9722 1200 www.mcwilliams.com.au	This historical cellar door is shaped like a wine barrel and built to exact scale, including the staves and hoops. Enjoy a picnic in idyllic surroundings on the vast lawns.

SOUTH AUSTRALIA

South Australia produces just under half of the grapes used to make Australia's wine. Adelaide, the state's capital city, is considered the focal point of the Australian wine industry, and is home to its major organisations and associations. Wine is integral to the South Australian economy, employing more people than any other industry. One of the reasons why South Australia enjoys both its preeminent status in Australian wine and the fact that most of the country's truly ancient vineyards are planted there is that is managed to avoid the scourge of phylloxera in the latter years of the nineteenth century.

Adelaide Hills

A surprisingly cool and very beautiful region immediately to the east of Adelaide and within a short drive of the city centre, the Adelaide Hills was initially South Australia's hub of apple and orchard fruit production. It first made a name for its sauvignon blanc, chardonnay

Bird in Hand Montepulciano 2014

Adelaide Hills

$30-$49

91/100

Musky, bright and fine-grained; dark cherries, chocolates and plums.

Hahndorf Hill Winery Gru Gruner Veltliner 2015

Adelaide Hills

$20-$29

92/100

Spicy, peppery peach/melon flavour; long, soft and chalky.

Lane Vineyard, The Gathering Sauvignon Blanc Semillon 2014

Adelaide Hills

$30-$49

94/100

Smoky and savoury, with gooseberry, melon and vanilla oak. Briny.

Michael Hall sang de pigeon Pinot Noir 2015

Adelaide Hills

$30-$49

90/100

Savoury, kernelly and slighly meaty, with faintly sour cherry/plum fruit.

Murdoch Hill Chardonnay 2015

Adelaide Hills

$20-$29

90/100

Peach, melon and grapefruit; smoky oak and a savoury finish.

chota barrels The int Vineyard hardonnay 14	**Penfolds Reserve Bin Chardonnay 2015**	**Pike & Joyce Sauvignon Blanc 2015**	**Riposte The Stiletto Pinot Gris 2015**	**Tapanappa Tiers Vineyard Chardonnay 2014**
delaide Hills	Adelaide Hills	Adelaide Hills	Adelaide Hills	Adelaide Hills
0-$49	$50-$99	$20-$29	$20-$29	$50-$99
/100	**95/100**	**92/100**	**90/100**	**95/100**
egant and cused, with onefruit, melon d a hint of stard.	Funky, wild and voluminous; long, taut and finely sculpted.	Pure, pristine and finely balanced; fresh gooseberries, lychees and dried herbs.	Spotless, fresh and focused, with a floral perfume and pear/apple fruit.	Spicy, floral and mineral; mouthfilling fruit and oak wrapped in brittle acids.

continued
Adelaide Hills

and riesling in the 1980s. It has also since became a popular source for sparkling base wines, while in recent times its warmer north-facing sites have shown great potential with the Rhône Valley varieties of shiraz and viognier. Newer entrants to Australian viticulture such as sangiovese, nebbiolo and grüner veltliner are making a home in this region.

JEREMY'S PICK OF ADELAIDE HILLS CELLAR DOORS

NAME	ADDRESS	CONTACT	SPECIAL FACILITIES
Golding Wines	52 Western Branch Road Lobethal SA 5241	08 8389 5120 peter@goldingwines.com.au www.goldingwines.com.au	Situated among vine-covered hills, guests can enjoy the park like areas surrounding the cellar door. Offering pizzas on weekends and regular Paella days, families and groups are welcome. Guests can participate in the Adopt A Vine program.
Lane Vineyard, The	5 Ravenswood Lane Hahndorf SA 5241	(08) 8388 1250 welcome@thelane.com.au www.thelane.com.au	Offers a range of experiences, such as 'Blend your Own' in the small batch winery, Heritage Vineyard Tour, Barrel Cellar Masterclass and the Gathering Indulgence wine and food experience.
Lane Vineyard, The	Pound Road Macclesfield SA 5153	08 8388 9694 cellardoor@longviewsa.com.au www.longviewvineyard.com.au	The long lunch takes on a new meaning with Sunday Tapas featuring sumptous platters designed to share with friends overlooking acres of undulating vineyards. Guests can stay in one of 12 self contained modern villas or the Homestead.
Shaw and Smith	136 Jones Road Balhannah SA 5242	(08) 8398 0500 admin@shawandsmith.com www.shawandsmith.com	Experience a selection of wines accompanied by a cheese sampler in the light filled tasting room overlooking the vines, hills and dam.

Barossa Valley

This famous South Australian region north of Adelaide is considered by many to be the heartbeat of Australian wine. Established from 1842 by a combination of migrant families from England and also from Silesia in Europe, the Barossa has developed its own identity more than any other Australian wine region. It is the only Australian region with its own entirely unique food culture and its Lutheran roots are proudly and happily evident throughout its charming collection of small towns and villages. The region

Burge Family Winemakers Olive Hill Semillon 2014

Barossa Valley

$20-$29

94/100

Melon, peach and citrus with restrained vanilla oak; long and focused.

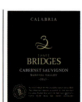

Calabria 3 Bridges Cabernet Sauvignon 2013

Barossa Valley

$20-$29

93/100

Handsomely oaked, with deep dark fruit, crunchy tannins and a savoury finish.

Hewitson Baby Bush Mourvèdre 2014

Barossa Valley

$20-$29

92/100

Luscious, fragrant and medium-bodied, with juicy berry/plum flavour.

Kalleske Buckboard Durif 2014

Barossa Valley

$20-$29

92/100

Floral and smoky; densely packed with dark berries and cherries.

Rockford Black Sparkling Shiraz 2015 disgorging

Barossa Valley

$50-$99

95/100

Wild, meaty and briary, with pastille-like dark fruits and fine tannins.

SOUTH AUSTRALIA

Saltram Winemaker's Selection Piano 2015

Barossa Valley

$20-$29

90/100

Herbal and floral, peachy and citrusy, with a savoury, lemon sherbet finish.

St Hallett Faith Shiraz 2014

Barossa Valley

$12-$19

90/100

Vibrant, peppery and spicy, with lively dark fruit and soft tannins.

Thorn Clarke Shotfire Shiraz 2014

Barossa Valley

$20-$29

91/100

Luscious, juicy and artfully oaked; with deep fruit and firmish tannins.

Torbreck Cuvée Juveniles Grenache Mataro Shiraz 2014

Barossa Valley

$20-$29

91/100

Spicy, floral and meaty, with smooth, juicy, licorice-like fruit.

Yalumba Old Bush Vine Grenache 2014

Barossa Valley

$20-$29

90/100

Medium-bodied, fragrant and spicy, with fresh blood plum flavour.

continued
Barossa Valley

is home to many of the grandest historic winery houses and buildings in this country.

A warm to hot region, the Barossa is responsible for many of the riper, more opulent expressions of Australian shiraz and grenache, plus many popular blends of these varieties with another red grape, mourvèdre (also called mataro). Its cabernet sauvignon can be sumptuous and long-living – especially from cooler vintages – but is rather less consistent. The Barossa's finest white wine is its brightly fruited, lightly herbal and gently oaked expression of semillon.

All indications would suggest that the Barossa Valley is dealing with its greatest challenges to date – those of climate change and the global trend to enjoy less densely packed and alcoholic red wines. As we see in many other leading Australian regions, there is today a focus on isolating the finest individual Barossa vineyards from which fruit is then harvested, vinified and marketed separately from larger volume labels.

JEREMY'S PICK OF BAROSSA VALLEY CELLAR DOORS

NAME	ADDRESS	CONTACT	SPECIAL FACILITIES
Charles Melton	Krondorf Road Tanunda SA 5352	(08) 8563 3606 cellardoor@ charlesmeltonwines.com.au www.charlesmeltonwines.com.au	Tastings are conducted around a large table in a cozy cellar door while the Locavore Lunch is served on the verandah overlooking the lawns. Guests can stay onsite in The Kirche, a beautifully restored 19th century church.
Kalleske	6 Murray Street Greenock SA 5360	(08) 8563 4000 wine@kalleske.com www.kalleske.com	Traditional Barossa platters and wine and food matching experiences available.
Seppeltsfield	730 Seppeltsfield Road Seppelstfield SA 5355	(08) 8568 6200 nicole@seppeltsfield.com.au www.seppeltsfield.com.au	This stunning historical property offers destination dining, VIP tastings overlooking the cellar door, 'Centennial Cellar' experiences, wine flights and heritage tours. Bike tours and adjacent Jam Factory hosting artisan craftspeople and designers complete the experience.
St Hugo	Barossa Valley Way Rowland Flat SA 5352	08 8115 9200 enquiries@sthugo.com www.sthugo.com	Stunning architecture, expansive decking, signature restaurant and underground private tasting room. Bespoke tours combine vineyard walks, tutored tastings and degustation experiences.

Clare Valley

North of the Barossa, amid rolling hills, native bushland and pastoral farming country is the picturesque Clare Valley, with its collection of small villages and historic old vineyards. Naturally beautiful and littered with some of Australia's most well-preserved stone buildings, Clare is a wonderful place to visit.

Annie's Lane Winemaker's Blend Cabernet Blend 2014

Clare Valley

$30-$49

93/100

Polished and elegant, with a charming length of sour-edged fruit.

Atlas Shiraz 2014

Clare Valley

$20-$29

92/100

Medium to full-bodied; earthy, brambly and generous, finishes savoury.

Grosset Springvale Riesling 2016

Clare Valley

$30-$49

95/100

Long and chalky, pristine and generous, laced with apple, pear and lemon.

Jim Barry The McRae Wood Shiraz 2014

Clare Valley

$30-$49

93/100

Smooth, supple and artfully balanced, charmingly peppery and elelgant.

Kilikanoon Mort's Reserve Riesling 2015

Clare Valley

$30-$49

96/100

Scented with apple blossom and lavender, long and pristin

SOUTH AUSTRALIA

Leasingham Classic Clare Riesling 2009

Clare Valley

$30-$49

95/100

Complex, toasty and developing; long and gentle, with trace of

Pauletts Helmsford Semillon 2015

Clare Valley

$20-$29

93/100

Generous, round and toasty; with juicy honeydew melon and gooseberry flavour.

Petaluma Hanlin Hill Riesling 2015

Clare Valley

$20-$29

94/100

Classically long and dry; with virbant, pear, apple and lime juice flavour.

Taylors Shiraz 2015

Clare Valley

$12-$19

89/100

Sweetly oaked, spicy and peppery; generous and mouthfilling.

Tim Adams The Fergus Grenache Blend 2013

Clare Valley

$20-$29

91/100

Spicy, floral and minty; firmish with juicy dark berry fruit.

continued
Clare Valley

Riesling is the region's speciality – a lusciously fruited and bone-dry wine that makes wonderful drinking either while very young or more mature. Slate outcrops add perfume to its bouquet and minerality to its texture. Clare semillon is juicy, long and vibrant.

Clare's shiraz is long, firm and minty, with layers of dense fruit and undertones of menthol. Its makers also specialise in rich, textured and age-worthy blends of cabernet sauvignon and malbec.

JEREMY'S PICK OF CLARE VALLEY CELLAR DOORS

NAME	ADDRESS	CONTACT	SPECIAL FACILITIES
Kilikanoon	Penna Lane Penwortham SA 5453	(08) 8843 4206 cellardoor@kilikanoon.com.au www.kilikanoon.com.au	Cellar door is located in an 1860's stone farmhouse surrounded by cottage gardens. Range of tasting experiences and cycling adventures available.
Paulett Wines	Sevehill-Mintaro Road Polish Hill River SA 5453	08 8843 4328 info@paulettwines.com.au www.paulettwines.com.au	Stunning rural views from the deck. Indigenous Australian bush food garden and Bush Devine Café offering a seasonal menu.
Sevenhill Cellars	111 College Road Sevenhill SA 5453	08 8843 4222 cellardoor@sevenhill.com.au www.sevenhill.com.au	Established in 1851 and Jesuit owned, featuring old stone winery, cellars, church, college buildings and spacious gardens. Guided and self-guided tours and cheese platters available. Ideal for families.
Skillogalee	Trevarrick Road Sevenhill SA 5453	(08) 8843 4311 info@skillogalee.com.au www.skillogalee.com.au	Handcrafted wines served in cottage surrounds with onsite restaurant and adjacent cottage accommodation.

Coonawarra

A cool to warm region in the southernmost extreme of South Australia, Coonawarra's vineyards are usually refreshed in the summer afternoons by cool sea breezes from the Southern Ocean. It is most famous for its finely balanced red wines, particularly those based around the cabernet sauvignon variety. Rarely above moderate richness, the finest of these are typically able to mature gracefully for several decades. Coonawarra's peppery, spicy shiraz is becoming equally popular. Medium to full in

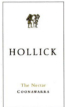

Hollick The Nectar Riesling 2014

Coonawarra

$20-$29

93/100

Honeyed and fragrant, long and luscious with apricot flavours and citrusy acids.

Leconfield Merlot 2014

Coonawarra

$20-$29

91/100

Restrained and gentle, with lively dark cherry and plum fruit.

Leconfield Old Vines Riesling 2015

Coonawarra

$20-$29

90/100

Lime juice, green apple skin and brittle acids, with a fine chalkiness.

Lindemans St George Cabernet Sauvignon 2014

Coonawarra

$50-$99

93/100

Scented with violets and cassis; long and firmish.

Majella Shiraz 2014

Coonawarra

$30-$49

90/100

Medium-weight, with jammy berry/plum fruit and crunchy tannins.

JEREMY'S PICK OF COONAWARRA CELLAR DOORS

NAME	ADDRESS	CONTACT	SPECIAL FACILITIES
Bellwether Wines	14183 Riddoch Hwy Coonawarra SA 5263	0417 080 945 sue@glenroywinemakers.com.au www.bellweatherwines.com.au	Featuring the renovated 1868 Glen Roy Shearing Shed, home to boutique winery, community kitchen, cellar door, produce garden and campground.
Hollick Estates	Corner Ravenswood Lane & Riddoch Highway Coonawarra SA 5263	08 8736 5001 admin@hollick.com www.hollick.com	Upstairs at Hollick restaurant offers contemporary Australian cuisine using regional produce sourced from the Limestone Coast. Vineyard tours also available.
Rymill Coonawarra	Riddoch Highway Coonawarra SA 5263	winery@rymill.com.au www.rymill.com.au	Offering a range of one-day inland foraging (Winter), two-day coastal foraging (Autumn) or all seasons 'Caves and Cabernet' experiences.
Wynns Coonawarra Estate	1 Memorial Drive Coonawarra SA 5263	(08) 8736 2225 www.wynns.com.au	Offering a "Make Your Own Blend' experience using Cabernet, Shiraz and Merlot varieties to produce your own personal bottle of wine.

continued Coonawarra

body, it's finer and often more savoury than many others from South Australia. At the heart of Coonawarra lies a cigar-shaped strip of thin red soil, known as terra rossa over solid limestone. The region's finest wines come from vineyards with a high proportion of this soil, which runs in a northerly direction from the town of Penola.

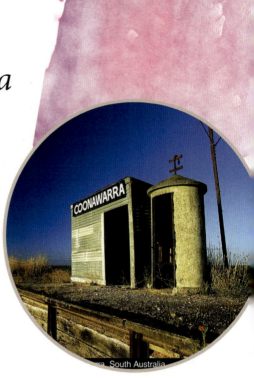

Parker Coonawarra Estate Terra Rossa First Growth Cabernet Blend 2012

Coonawarra

$100-$199

95/100

Elegant, long and stylish, with pristine dark fruits and tight-grained tannins.

Penfolds Bin 128 Shiraz 2014

Coonawarra

$30-$49

92/100

Floral, spicy and brightly lit with small dark berries, soft and velvety.

Redman Cabernet Sauvignon 2014

Coonawarra

$30-$49

95/100

Pristine and floral, with palate-staining fruit and gravelly

St Hugo Cabernet Sauvignon 2013

Coonawarra

$30-$49

95/100

Piercingly intense, long, robust and fine-grained. Give it

Wynns Coonawarra Estate Shiraz 2014

Coonawarra

$12-$19

91/100

Smooth and silky, laced with pepper and spice, elegant and faintly herbal.

Eden Valley

Culminating at the peak of the High Eden Valley, the rolling, rocky hills to the east of the Barossa Valley are known as the Eden Valley. Their principal wines are the chalky, citrusy and perfumed dry rieslings that can live for decades, plus silky, fine-grained and deeply-fruited reds from shiraz and cabernet sauvignon, which reveal powerful mulberry and cassis-like flavours. The shiraz is typically very spicy and peppery, while the cabernet sauvignon often reveals undertones of dried herbs and dark chocolate.

Henschke Mount Edelstone Shiraz 2012

Eden Valley

$100-$199

95/100

Elegant, smooth and silky, with a peppery presence of dark berries and plums.

Mountadam Patriarch Shiraz 2012

High Eden

$30-$49

95/100

Long and velvety, with plush dark berries and plums, smoky

Penfolds Bin 51 Riesling 2016

Eden Valley

$30-$49

90/100

Penetrative and pure, with fresh lemon juice and green apple skin character.

Peter Lehmann H&V Eden Valley Riesling 2015

Eden Valley

$20-$29

94/100

Floral and mineral, with a long palate of citrus and green apple skin flavour.

Yalumba Hand Picked Shiraz Viognier 2012

Eden Valley

$30-$49

93/100

Briary, floral and meaty; long, gentle and piercingly intense.

JEREMY'S PICK OF EDEN VALLEY CELLAR DOORS

NAME	ADDRESS	CONTACT	SPECIAL FACILITIES
Fernfield Wines	112 Rushlea Road Eden Valley SA 5235	0422 296 221 scott@fernfieldwines.com.au www.fernfieldwines.com.au	Offering intimate tasting experiences in an 1856 settler's cottage, including chocolate pairing, 'Play the Winemaker' blending session and gourmet platters featuring freshly baked bread.
	1428 Keyneton Road Keyneton SA 5353	(08) 8564 8223 info@henschke.com.au www.henschke.com.au	VIP Tours and Tastings take visitors into the historic working winery, through the renowned Hill of Grace vineyard and into the private cellar for an intimate tastings. Bookings essential.
Taste Eden Valley	6 Washington Street Angaston SA 5353	08 8564 2435 info@tasteedenvalley.com.au www.tasteedenvalley.com.au	Experience a range of different Eden Valley producers in the one tasting room.
Edenmae Estate Cellar Door	7 Miller Street Springton SA 5235	08 8568 2098 wine@edenmae.com.au www.edenmae.com.au	Small family-run boutique winery offering tastings, sales by the glass, local platters and organic coffee. Vinestay B&B is a rustic family friendly cottage at the mixed farming Edenmae Estate at Mount Pleasant.

McLaren Vale

A warm, maritime region immediately south of Adelaide, McLaren Vale is best known for its luscious, smooth and sour-edged shirazes, which often deliver deep, powerful flavours of blackberries, plums, olives and bitumen. Typically, they are not strongly astringent, so they are usually very approachable while young. McLaren Vale is also showing great potential with the Italian varieties of sangiovese and nebbiolo, plus the Spanish variety of tempranillo.

   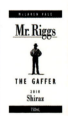

Angove Warboys Vineyard Grenache 2014
McLaren Vale
$30-$49
91/100
Luscious, smooth and fragrant, with bright berry fruit and a cola note.

Coriole Fiano 2015
McLaren Vale
$20-$29
91/100
Citrus and melon backed by clove and oregano. Nervy acids.

d'Arenberg d'Arry's Original Shiraz Grenache 2013
McLaren Vale
$12-$19
92/100
Dark-fruited and spicy, fine and kernelly, with a lingering finish.

Mitolo Angela Shiraz 2014
McLaren Vale
$30-$49
95/100
Gentle, floral and silky, but pristine and penetrative.

Mr Riggs The Gaffer Shiraz 2014
McLaren Vale
$20-$29
92/100
Vibrant and peppery, medium-bodied with intense dark fruit.

continued McLaren Vale

Oliver's Taranga Vermentino 2015

McLaren Vale

$20-$29

91/100

Zesty and citrusy, with pear/apple fruit and hints of sage.

Penny's Hill Cracking Black Shiraz 2014

McLaren Vale

$20-$29

91/100

Brightly lit, peppery and translucent, with berry/plum fruit and a mineral finish.

Primo Estate Joseph 'Moda' Cabernet Sauvignon Merlot 2014

McLaren Vale

$50-$99

95/100

Long, firm and crunchy, with a deep, seamless palate.

Reynella Basket Pressed Shiraz 2014

McLaren Vale

$50-$99

97/100

Truly remarkable: floral and deeply fruited; tight-grained and smoky.

Wirra Wirra Church Block Cabernet Shiraz Merlot 2014

McLaren Vale

$20-$29

90/100

Spicy, peppery and floral, with bright fruit and fresh oak.

JEREMY'S PICK OF McLAREN VALE CELLAR DOORS

NAME	ADDRESS	CONTACT	SPECIAL FACILITIES
Beresford Wines	252 Blewitt Springs Road McLaren Flat SA 5171	08 8383 0362 info@beresfordwines.com.au www.beresfordwines.com.au	Stunning tasting pavilion where guests can choose their tasting experience matched with tasting plate of seasonal, local produce. Food and wine matching classes and educational sessions available.
d'Arenberg	1 Osborn Road McLaren Vale SA 5171	(08) 8329 4888 www.darenberg.com.au	Choose from a range of adventures: interactive blending experience, masterclasses, 4wd tours and scenic flights. Dine in style at d'Arry's Verandah Restaurant.
Gemtree Wines	167 Elliott Road McLaren Flat SA 5171	08 8323 0802 info@gemtreewines.com www.gemtreewines.com.au	Sustainable Cellar Door with extensive deck and lawn areas. Organic produce platters, playground and activities for children, Art Space and Wetlands Ecotrail.
Primo Estate	50 McMurtrie Road McLaren Vale SA 5171	(08) 8323 6800 info@primoestate.com.au www.primoestate.com.au	Premium Joseph wines served with crusty bread, Italian cheese and Joseph EVOO served in the architecturally stunning cellar door.

TASMANIA

Australia's smallest and southernmost state, Tasmania is now home to a steadily maturing and expanding wine industry. Its southerly latitude provides its wine regions with longer hours of sunshine per day than regions on the Australian mainland, which is an important factor behind the quality of its sparkling wines and dry red pinot noirs. Tasmania's wines are less obviously Australian in style, and often reveal some of the perfume and delicacy associated with European wines.

Coal River Valley

Despite its southerly latitude, this region is one of the warmer locations in Tasmania. While it needs a warmer season to produce truly outstanding cabernet sauvignon, it is perhaps more consistent with its pinot noir, riesling and very dusty, heady and piercingly intense sauvignon blanc. It is found just north of the Tasmanian capital of Hobart.

Domaine A Petit a Cabernet Blend 2010
Coal River Valley
$50-$99
94/100
Complex, old school and cigarboxy; long and elegant.

Frogmore Creek Riesling 2014
Coal River Valley
$20-$29
93/100
Austere and mouthfilling, with a floral perfume and undertones of bath powder.

Heemskerk Coal River Valley Chardonnay 2015
Coal River Valley
$30-$49
94/100
Floral, funky and artfully made; elegant and savoury.

Pooley Pinot Noir 2014
Coal River Valley
$30-$49
92/100
Smooth, seamless and evenly ripened, steeped in cherry/plum fruit.

Tolpuddle Pinot Noir 2014
Coal River Valley
$50-$99
95/100
Heady, fragrant, smooth and supple, with pristine berry and cherry

JEREMY'S PICK OF COAL RIVER VALLEY CELLAR DOORS

NAME	ADDRESS	CONTACT	SPECIAL FACILITIES
Domaine A/Stoney Vineyard	105 Tea Tree Road Campania Tas 7026	(03) 6260 4174 althaus@domaine-a.com.au www.domaine-a.com.au	Listed as 'Outstanding' by Langton's and sought after by collectors, this winery also produced Tasmania's first fine wine brandy.
Frogmore Creek	699 Richmond Road Cambridge Tas 7170	(03) 6248 4484 admin@frogmorecreek.com.au www.frogmorecreek.com.au	Home to four brands: Frogmore Creek, Meadowbank, Storm Bay and 42 Degrees South, the venue includes tasting room, gallery and restaurant.
Riversdale Estate	222 Denholms Road Cambridge Tas 7170	(03) 6248 5555 info@riversdaleestate.com.au www.riversdaleestate.com.au	The French Bistro serves lunch daily or guests can enjoy High Tea in the Orangery. Stay the night in one of 7 luxury French Provincial Cottages. Children can visit Peter Rabbit's Garden.
Pooley Wines	1431 Richmond Road Richmond Tas 7025	(03) 6260 2895 enquiries@pooleywines.com.au www.pooleywines.com.au	This fully accredited environmentally sustainable winery offers wine flights in historic Belmont House. Enjoy a BYO platter or picnic in family friendly surroundings.

East Coast

A very small region, with some excellent vineyard sites sheltered from prevailing westerly winds. The best of these sites capture sunshine through much of the day, and can make excellent wines from a surprisingly wide range of varieties that includes pinot noir, chardonnay and riesling.

Cape Bernier Pinot Noir 2010

East Coast

$30-$49

92/100

Musky and floral, with meaty berry/cherry fruit and notes of underbrush.

Freycinet Chardonnay 2015

East Coast

$30-$49

94/100

Peach, pear, apple and melon backed by creamy, nutty oak. Finishes fresh.

Freycinet Louis Pinot Noir 2015

East Coast

$30-$49

93/100

Juicy and brightly lit, with fresh dark cherry/berry fruit and fine tannins.

Radenti Chardonnay Pinot Noir 2011

East Coast

$50-$99

95/100

Perfumed and floral, with tangy citrus/melon fruit and a mineral

Spring Vale Melrose Pinot Noir 2016

East Coast

$20-$29

89/100

Heady and floral with raspberry bubblegum fruit, fresh acids and little firmness.

JEREMY'S PICK OF EAST COAST CELLAR DOORS

NAME	ADDRESS	CONTACT	SPECIAL FACILITIES
Spring Vale	130 Spring Vale Road Cranbrook Tas 7190	(03) 6257 8208 rodney@springvalewines.com www.springvalewines.com	These Pinot Noir specialists offer wine tasting in an original convict-built stable as well as a vineyard seafood restaurant open daily.
Devil's Corner	Sherbourne Road Apslawn Tas 7190	(03) 6257 8881 www.brownbrothers.com.au/about-us/our-brands/devils-corner	The Cellar Door is surrounded by magnificent views of 'The Hazards' on the Freycinet Peninsular and Moulting Lagoon, a wetland of international environmental significance.
Freycinet	15919 Tasman Highway Bicheno Tas 7215	(03) 6257 8574 info@freycinetvineyard.com.au www.brownbrothers.com.au/about-us/our-brands/devils-corner	Very picturesque. Wine tours are available by appointment
Priory Ridge	280 Ansons Bay Road St Helens Tas 7216	(03) 6376 1916 info@prioryridgewines.com www.prioryridgewines.com	This winery offers a unique experience where a range of premium cool climate wines can be tasted at their rustic Cellar door.

Pipers River

A cool northerly region in Tasmania that has emerged since the early 1980s to become one of Australia's principal sources of high quality sparkling wines and some of its most fragrant and exotic riesling, pinot gris and gewürztraminer. Like most Tasmanian regions, it also excels with pinot noir and chardonnay table wines.

Bay of Fires Pinot Noir 2014

Tasmania

$30-$49

95/100

Pristine, heady and finely balanced; long, pliant and faintly sappy.

Dalrymple Cave Block Chardonnay 2014

Pipers River

$30-$49

93/100

Scented with smoked meats and ginger; long, soft and luscious.

Delamere Vineyards Pinot Noir 2014

Pipers River

$30-$49

92/100

Floral and faintly herbal; long and balanced, waiting to build.

Jansz asmania Vintage Rosé 2011

Pipers River

$30-$49

91/100

Meaty, with aromas of small red fruit and orange candy; creamy and savoury.

Pipers Brook Estate Gewürztraminer 2014

Pipers River

$30-$49

90/100

Musky scents of lychees and rose oil; slightly oily and briny to finish.

JEREMY'S PICK OF PIPERS RIVER CELLAR DOORS

NAME	ADDRESS	CONTACT	SPECIAL FACILITIES
Bay of Fires	40 Baxters Road Pipers Brook Tas 7254	(03) 6382 7622 info@ dalrymplevineyards. com.au www. dalrymplevineyards. com.au	Guests can experience tastings in the award winning modern, architecturally-designed building surrounded by established gardens, the vines, the winery and Pipers River.
Delamere	4238 Bridport Road Pipers Brook Tas 7254	(03) 6382 7190 shane@ delamerevineyards. com.au www. delamerevineyards. com.au	Families are encouraged to try a BYO picnic to enjoy the scenery of the vineyard whilst tasting the Sparkling wines, Pinot Noir, Chardonnay and "Naissante" range of wines at the cellary door.
Jansz Tasmania	1216B Pipers Brook Road Pipers Brook Tas 7254	(03) 6382 7066 info@jansz.com.au www.jansz.com.au	The Jansz Tasmania Wine Room which is located next to the vineyard offers guests the opportunity to taste the Sparkling range while overlooking a picturesque lake.
Leaning Church	76 Brooks Road Lalla Tas 7267	(03) 6395 4447 www.leaningchurch. com.au	Wine tastings can be enjoyed with lunch from the Restaurant as well as Hellyers Road single malt whisky tastings and tours of the historic leaning church

Tamar Valley

Another northern Tasmanian region capable of high-quality wines from the Burgundian, Alsatian and Champagne varieties. Sited alongside the picturesque Tamar River and estuary north of Launceston, its wine producers are typically small and aspirational.

Grey Sands Pinot Gris 2014

Tamar Valley

$30-$49

90/100

Complex and meaty, laced with cloves, nougat and honeysuckle.

Holm Oak Pinot Noir 2014

Tamar Valley

$30-$49

93/100

Elegant and perfumed, musky and exotic, long and silky.

Leo Buring Leopold Riesling 2015

Tamar Valley

$30-$49

95/100

Very Germanic, with pristine stonefruit scents; long, finely balance and off-dry.

Moorilla Muse Series Cabernet Sauvignon Blend 2013

Tamar Valley

$30-$49

94/100

Firmish, drying and faintly minty, with plummy fruit

Tamar Ridge Reserve Pinot Noir 2013

Tamar Valley

$50-$99

92/100

Long and gentle with musky scents of cherry blossom.

JEREMY'S PICK OF TAMAR VALLEY CELLAR DOORS

NAME	ADDRESS	CONTACT	SPECIAL FACILITIES
Josef Chromy	370 Relbia Road Relbia Tas 7258	(03) 6335 8700 wine@josefchromy.com.au www.josefchromy.com.au	This 1880s homestead surrounded by established gardens offers wine tasting in front of an open log fire and boasts an award-winning restaurant.
Holm Oak Vineyard	11 West Bay Road Rowella Tas 7270	(03) 6394 7577 admin@holmoakvineyards.com.au www.holmoakvineyards.com.au	Guests can visit Pinot d'Pig and feed him a few apples on their way to the Cellar Door to create a platter or picnic with local cheese, terrines and salmon products with the wine tastings.
Moore's Hill	3343 West Tamar Highway Sidmouth Tas 7270	(03) 6394 7649 www.mooreshill.com.au	The Cellar Door offers local produce tasting platters to share with the wine tastnings, as well as a Tasmanian whisky flight.
Marion's Vineyard	335 Foreshore Road Deviot Tas 7275	(03) 6394 7434 accomm@marionsvineyard.com.au www.marionsvineyard.com.au	A spectacular and sustainable vineyard running right down to the west bank of the Tamar houses a small, elevated cellar door with stunning views. Accommodation available.

TASMANIA

VICTORIA

While much of inland and northern Victoria is historically hot and dry, it boasts a number of high quality wine regions in cooler areas to the south of the state. Victoria has more climatic and geological diversity with quality viticultural land than other states, and as a consequence has the largest collection of wine regions. Its capital city, Melbourne, is widely regarded as Australia's centre of food and wine culture.

Beechworth/ Alpine Valleys

A cool to warm region high in the Victorian Alps, Beechworth is becoming best known for its heady, peppery and exotically perfumed shiraz, which is typically made in the more savoury European style. Cooler south-facing sites are deployed to make some wonderfully sumptuous chardonnay and spicy pinot noir. Varieties such as roussanne and gamay are also showing some promise. The Alpine Valleys vineyards are planted at a higher altitude, and develop more fragrant, delicate styles.

Castagna Adam's Rib The Red 2013
Beechworth
$30-$49
94/100
Tarry, meaty and earthy; a charming and savoury blend of nebbiolo and shiraz.

Giaconda Nantua les Deux Chardonnay 2015
Beechworth
$50-$99
93/100
Complex and nougat-like, with melon/grapefurit flavour and matchstick oak.

Giaconda Estate Shiraz 2014
Beechworth
$100-$199
97/100
Powerful, evolving and meaty, with layers of fruit and minerality.

Sorrenberg Gamay 2014
Beechworth
$30-$49
91/100
Bright redcurrant, cola and cherry flavours with fine tannins and fresh acids.

Star Lane Quattro Vitigni 2014
Beechworth
$30-$49
93/100
Firm and savoury, with sour-edged fruit and meaty complexity.

JEREMY'S PICK OF BEECHWORTH/ALPINE VALLEYS CELLAR DOORS

NAME	ADDRESS	CONTACT	SPECIAL FACILITIES
Amulet Wines	1036 Wangaratta Road Beechworth Vic 3747	(03) 5727 0420 sales@amuletwines.com.au www.amuletwines.com.au	This delightful glass walled cellar door offers seasonal a la carte lunches featuring regional produce.
Feathertop	6619 Great Alpine Road Porepunkah Vic 3740	(03) 5756 2356 boynton@boynton.com.au www.boynton.com.au	Boasting a restaurant, deli and spa, plus 2 apartments for lease, this is also a busy event venue.
Giaconda	30 McClay Road Everton Upper Vic 3678	(03) 5727 0246 info@giaconda.com.au www.giaconda.com.au	Iconic wines are aged deep underground in a granite maturation cave. Wines are highly sought after and visits are by appointment only.
Indigo Wine Company	1221 Beechworth-Wangaratta Road Everton Upper Vic 3678	(03) 5727 0233 emails@indigovineyard.com.au www.indigovineyard.com.au	Rustic cellar door featuring structured wine tastings, open fire and tasting plate. Experience the 4km Indigo Vineyard Mountain Bike Trail or relax over bocce on the lawn.

Geelong

An historic region whose vineyards were wiped out by phylloxera more than a century ago, Geelong is located to the south and west of Melbourne. Its diverse mixture of sites lends it to a wide range of wines, of which shiraz, pinot noir and chardonnay have registered the greatest success. Geelong's elegant red wines typically deliver deep, powerful aromas and are rarely heavy or extracted.

Clyde Park Single Block B3 Chardonnay 2015

Geelong

$50-$99

92/100

Long, bright and fresh, with penetrative citrus and pineapple fruit.

Del Rios Shiraz 2015

Geelong

$30-$49

91/100

Spicy and peppery, with intense flavours of cassis, cola and blood plum.

Hildegard Dry White 2015

Geelong

$30-$49

92/100

Pristine, fragrant and focused, with fresh apple, peach and pear fruit.

Lethbridge Mietta Pinot Noir 2012

Geelong

$50-$99

89/100

Rustic and meaty, firm and drying but likely to flesh out.

Paradise IV Chardonnay 2015

Geelong

$50-$99

97/100

Complex, funky and floral; long and luxuriant, finishing mineral

JEREMY'S PICK OF GEELONG CELLAR DOORS

NAME	ADDRESS	CONTACT	SPECIAL FACILITIES
Lethbridge Wines	74 Burrows Road Lethbridge Vic 3332	(03) 5281 7279 info@lethbridgewines.com www.lethbridgewines.com	Intimate tasting experience in winery constructed of strawbales. Meredith Dairy Cheese available for sampling and sale.
Leura Park Estate	1400 Portarlington Road Curlewis Vic 3222	(03) 5253 3180 www.leuraparkestate.com.au	Quirky architectural cellar door design is reminiscent of the Sydney Opera House. Features guided tastings, sensational food served alfresco or by the roaring fires in Winter. Live music on Sundays and Segway Tours available.
McGlashans Wallington Estate	225 Swan Bay Road Wallington Vic 3221	(03) 5250 5760 mcglash@pipeline www.mcglashans.com.au	New cellar door offering a range of fresh, gourmet food platters. Classic Cars & Maritime Exhibition open every weekend.
Oakdene Vineyards & Restaurant	255 Grubb Road Wallington Vic 3221	(03) 5256 3886 info@oakdene.com.au www.oakdene.com.au	Located in the 'Upside-Down House' guests can enjoy a tutored wine tasting, browse the retail shop or stroll through the art gardens. Onsite restaurant and café caters for all day dining and homestead accommodation is available.

Grampians/ Great Western

In the southern part of western Victoria, a landscape dominated by extinct volcanoes, this small but very significant region makes some of Australia's most sought-after shiraz. Known for its intense dark pepper character, the purity of its fruit and the fineness of its tannins, Grampians Great Western shiraz is a unique and long-living wine that develops wonderful complexity with age. The region can also produce very floral and crystal-clear riesling.

Best's Great Western Bin No. '0' Shiraz 2014

Grampians Great Western

$50-$99

94/100

Classically musky, spicy and deeply flavoured; elegant and

Montara Gold Rush Riesling 2015

Grampians Great Western

$20-$29

90/100

Floral and fragrant, long and chalky, marginally sweet.

Mount Langi Ghiran Cliff Edge Shiraz 2014

Grampians Great Western

$30-$49

92/100

Vivacious black and blue fruits, balanced and gentle, lingering finish.

Mountainside Nebbiolo 2015

Grampians Great Western

$20-$29

92/100

Earthy, meaty and savoury, with blood plum and citrus, fresh acids.

Seppelt St Peters Shiraz 2014

Grampians Great Western

$50-$99

94/100

Elegant, smooth and stylish, with sweetly oaked red and black fruits.

JEREMY'S PICK OF GRAMPIANS/GREAT WESTERN CELLAR DOORS

NAME	ADDRESS	CONTACT	SPECIAL FACILITIES
Best's Great Western	111 Bests Road Great Western Vic 3374	(03) 5356 2250 info@bestswines.com www.bestswines.com.	Established in the mid 1860's, this truly memorable historical cellar door includes hand-dug cellars for visitors to discover during the Cellar Walk.
Grampians Estate	1477 Western Highway Great Western Vic 3374	003 5356 2400 info@grampiansestate.com.au www.grampiansestate.com.au	Kick back on a sofa, enjoy freshly prepared cheese platters, muffins and peruse the selection of local produce and other collectables. Picnic tables and electric bbq available.
Mount Langi Ghiran	80 Vine Road Bayindeen Vic 3375	(03) 5354 3207 info@langi.com.au www.langi.com.au	Set by a magnificent mountain backdrop, visitors are encouraged to bring a picnic hamper and enjoy the property. Blankets, cushions and glasses are provided, while other activities include bocce, biking and table tennis.
Montara Wines	76 Chalambar Road Ararat Vic 3377	(03) 5352 3868 cellardoor@montarawines.com.au www.montarawines.com.au	Built from 90 year old mud bricks and other salvaged materials, guests can enjoy a tasting at the bar made from old champagne riddling racks. Onsite café offers fresh local produce.

Heathcote

A relatively new region immediately to the north of Melbourne, Heathcote has become a shiraz specialist. With a distinctive and rare outcrop of 100 million year-old Cambrian soil and greenstone beneath many of its vineyards, Heathcote's shiraz varies between a fragrant and savoury style and a more opulent and lavishly fruited expression that reflects the very high levels of ripeness sought after by many growers.

Brown Brothers Heathcote Durif 2014

Heathcote

$20-$29

90/100

Briary and floral, with restrained black and blue fruits, cedary oak.

Jasper Hill Georgia's Paddock Shiraz 2014

Heathcote

$50-$99

95/100

Dense, dark, chocolatey and meaty; with assertive fruit and firm tannins.

Pyrette Shiraz 2015

Heathcote

$30-$49

93/100

Peppery, floral and spicy, medium-bodied, gentle and savoury.

Seppelt Mount Ida Shiraz 2014

Heathcote

$50-$99

92/100

Dark-fruited, minty and peppery; firm and drying, mineral finish.

Vinea Marson Viognier 2014

Heathcote

$30-$49

94/100

Spotlessly pure, long and savoury; musky, spicy and floral.

JEREMY'S PICK OF HEATHCOTE CELLAR DOORS

NAME	ADDRESS	CONTACT	SPECIAL FACILITIES
Heathcote Winery	185 High Street Heathcote Vic 3523	(03) 5433 2595 www.heathcotewinery.com.au	A shady courtyard provides the ideal place to enjoy a light meal from the Galleria with a glass of wine. Large range of gourment produce, glassware and accessories also available.
Merindoc Café & Cellar Door	2905 Lancefield-Tooborac Road Tooborac Vic 3522	03 5433 5188 café@merindochq.com.au www.merindoc.com.au	Featuring fresh produce from the kitchen garden, the seasonal weekend menu goes perfectly with the Shelmerdine family's wines. Cottage accommodation available neary.
Vinea Marson	411 Heathcote Rochester Road Mount Camel Vic 3523	0400 865 524 hello@vineamarson www.vineamarson.com	Tastings are held in true Italian style - with food at the Marson family table. Tastings by appointment.
McIvor Estate	80 Tooborac-Baynton Road Tooborac Vic 3522	03 5433 5266 info@mcivorestate.com.au www.mcivorestate.com.au	Overlooking the vineyard and olive grove, visitors can sample pizza and fresh baked bread from the wood-fired oven then work it off over a game of bocce.

Mornington Peninsula

A maritime holiday region southeast of Melbourne surrounded by sea on three sides, the Mornington Peninsula is maturing as a serious producer of pinot noir and chardonnay. Its pinot noirs are typically heady, perfumed and spicy, with deep, accentuated fruit characters. Higher sites around Red Hill produce wines of more delicacy and subtlety. Pinot gris has also become a popular wine within this region.

Hurley Vineyard Garamond Pinot Noir 2014

Mornington Peninsula

$50-$99

96/100

Heady, floral and smoky, with lustrous fruit and fine, firmish tannins.

Kooyong Beurrot Pinot Gris 2015

Mornington Peninsula

$30-$49

93/100

Complex, musky and spicy; like a luscious white Turkish delight.

Moorooduc Estate Chardonnay 2014

Mornington Peninsula

$30-$49

92/100

Smooth, creamy and waxy, with bright peach, melon and pineapple flavour.

Port Phillip Estate Sauvignon 2015

Mornington Peninsula

$20-$29

93/100

Lightly oaked and herbal; gooseberries, passionfruit and mineral.

Red Claw Pinot Noir 2015

Mornington Peninsula

$20-$29

90/100

Generous and round, with mouthfilling plum, beetroot and cola flavour.

VICTORIA

orret
Ilnarring
not Noir
15

ornington
eninsula

0-$49

/100

ral and
thy, with
araschino
erry fruit
apped in
vy acids.

Stonier
Reserve
Chardonnay
2014

Mornington
Peninsula

$30-$49

95/100

Spicy, smoky
and floral; long,
elegant and
briny.

William
Downie
Mornington
Peninsula
Pinot Noir
2015

Mornington
Peninsula

$50-$99

91/100

Wild and
meaty, with
searingly
intense sour-
edged fruit.

Willow Creek
Vineyard Pinot
Noir 2014

Mornington
Peninsula

$30-$49

93/100

Supple,
long and
very gentle;
perfumed and
elegant.

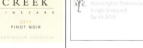

Yabby Lake
Single
Vineyard
Syrah 2015

Mornington
Peninsula

$20-$29

91/100

Savoury, meaty
and Rhône-
inspired; long,
peppery and
gentle.

JEREMY'S PICK OF MORNINGTON PENINSULA CELLAR DOORS

NAME	ADDRESS	CONTACT	SPECIAL FACILITIES
Crittenden Estate	25 Harrisons Road Dromana Vic 3936	(03) 5987 3800 winecentre@crittendenwines.com.au www.crittendenwines.com.au	Experienced a relaxed wine flight served by knowledgeable staff in a contemporary cellar door. Restaurant and accommodation also available on the property.
Foxey's Hangout	795 White Hill Road Red Hill Vic 3937	(03) 5989 2022 info@foxeys-hangout.com.au www.foxeys-hangout.com.au	Join the winemaker and observe the the final stages of making fine sparkling wine. Guests can select their own dosage and take home a bottle of sparkling they've designed to suit their personal palate.
Montalto	33 Shoreham Road Red Hill South Vic 3937	(03) 5989 8412 info@montalto.com.au www.montalto.com.au	Spend an entire day enjoying this beautiful property. Whether it's taking a Wetlands Walk through vines, gardens and scuplture, indulging in gourmet food or exceptional wine experiences that combine golf or behind-the-scenes tours.
Port Phillip Estate	263 Red Hill Road Red Hill South Vic 3937	(03) 5989 4444 cd@portphillipestate.com.au www.portphillipestate.com.au	Stunning property oerlooking the lake with sophisticated dining and masterclasses for groups. Six contemporary suites available for those looking to stay overnight in a winery.

Pyrenees

A cool to warm area in the west of central Victoria, the Pyrenees became an important wine region during the 1970s. Spread across lands that were mined for gold in the nineteenth century, the Pyrenees vineyards are mainly found near the settlements of Avoca, Moonambel and Redbank. The region is unusually picturesque, with the Pyrenees mountains providing a number of cooler and protected viticultural sites, often in close proximity to mature eucalypt forest. The region's best wine is red, from the Bordeaux varieties as well as shiraz, although it can produce fine sparkling wine, especially from chardonnay. It's a peaceful, rural region, without large crowds of tourists, making it a wonderful place to visit.

Blue Pyrenees Estate Cabernet Blend 2013

Pyrenees

$30-$49

94/100

Floral, firm and deeply flavoured, long and cigarboxy. Classic.

Blue Pyrenees Midnight Cuvée 2012

Pyrenees

$30-$49

91/100

Fresh and fragrant, with a fine bead and a long, creamy, peachy palate.

Dalwhinnie Moonambel Chardonnay 2014

Pyrenees

$30-$49

89/100

Smooth and creamy, with juicy nectarine, melon and citrusy fruit.

Redbank Winery Sally's Paddock Cabernet Blend 2013

Pyrenees

$50-$99

96/100

Classically firm, layered and measured, steeped in fruit, for the cellar.

Taltarni Estate Cabernet Sauvignon 2013

Pyrenees

$30-$49

94/100

For the long term, with pristine, minty cassis, dark plum and mulberry flavou

JEREMY'S PICK OF PYRENEES CELLAR DOORS

NAME	ADDRESS	CONTACT	SPECIAL FACILITIES
Blue Pyrenees Estate	Vinoca Road Avoca Vic 3467	(03) 5465 1111 info@bluepyrenees.com.au www.bluepyrenees.com.au	A friendly cellar door and fine country restaurant with wine and food pairings and cellar door exclusive releases.
Redbank Winery	1926 Sunraysia Highway Redbank Vic 3477	(03) 5467 7255 sales@sallyspaddock.com.au www.sallyspaddock.com.au	Taste current and back releases, enjoy and ploughman's lunch at the Flying Pig Deli or settle in for a few days at the mud brick cottage.
Taltarni	339 Taltarni Road Moonambel Vic 3478	(03) 5459 7900 info@taltarni.com.au www.taltarni.com.au	Enjoy a tasting surrounded by eucalypt forest and vineyards, challenge your friends at petanque or stage an intimate dinner in the cellar cave.
Warrenmang	188 Mountain Creek Road Moonambel Vic 3478	(03) 5467 2233 bazzani@warrenmang.com.au www.warrenmang.com.au	Tastings, tours and a renowned restaurant at the chalet-styled Warrenmang resort. A long-time favoured destination for those wanting to escape.

Rutherglen

An historic warm to hot region in the northeast of Victoria, Rutherglen is home to an incomparable collection of Australian fortified wines. Based on the varieties of shiraz, frontignac and muscadelle, they are the most concentrated, luscious and complex of their kind in Australia. Rutherglen is also known for its moderately rich, smooth and earthy shiraz, as well as its meaty, savoury and astringent durif.

All Saints Estate Marsanne 2015
Rutherglen
$20-$29
90/100
Smooth, spicy and floral, with melon and nougat wrapped in citrusy acids.

Anderson Verrier Durif Shiraz 2008
Rutherglen
$30-$49
91/100
Wild and rustic, with a fiery core of meaty ripe dark berry/plum flavour.

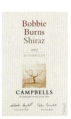

Campbells Bobbie Burns Shiraz 2014
Rutherglen
$20-$29
91/100
Full-flavoured, smooth and generous, with rich, meaty fruit.

Campbells Trebbiano 2014
Rutherglen
$12-$19
88/100
Crisp, clean, delicate and floral, with peach/apple fruit and lively acids.

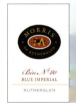

Morris Bin No 80 Blue Imperial 2014
Rutherglen
$12-$19
89/100
Firm and rustic, rather drying and raw; needs plenty of time.

JEREMY'S PICK OF RUTHERGLEN CELLAR DOORS

NAME	ADDRESS	CONTACT	SPECIAL FACILITIES
All Saints Estate	315 All Saints Road Wahgunyah Vic 3687	(02) 6035 2222 customerservice@allsaintswine.com.au www.allsaintswine.com.au	From private wine tastings and historical winery tours, winemaker for a day and gourmet experiences to indulgent weekend escapes, all visitors and families are catered for at this genuine wine tourism destination.
Campbells	4603 Murray Valley Highway Rutherglen Vic 3685	(02) 6033 6000 sales@campbellswines.com.au www.campbellswines.com.au	Perfectly aged Muscats and Topaques are hallmarks of this great vineyard. Visitors can explore the cellars, participate in a guided tour or private tastings or indulge in a Hamper box filled with regional produce.
Cofield Wines	Distillery Road Wahgunyah Vic 3687	(02) 6033 3798 www.cofieldwines.com.au	Experience Grapevine Glamping by staying in the Cofield vineyards. By day enjoy wine flights and gourmet produce from Pickled Sisters Café.
Jones Winery & Vineyard	61 Jones Road Rutherglen Vic 3685	(02) 6032 8496 jones@joneswinery.com.au www.joneswinery.com.au	Boutique cellar door and café serving French inspired café dishes and picnic hampers.

Yarra Valley

Another region close to Melbourne, this time due east from the city, the Yarra Valley is another historic Victorian wine region dating back to the 1840s. Its rebirth in the 1970s saw a renewed focus on pinot noir and chardonnay, plus the development of some of Australia's most elegant and long-living blends of cabernet sauvignon and merlot. Recent years have seen the expansion into warmer sites, with some very exciting developments around shiraz and viognier.

Coldstream Hills Deer Farm Vineyard Pinot Gris 2015

Yarra Valley

$30-$49

91/100

Fresh pear, apple and peach laced with scents of white flowers and cinnamon.

Dominique Portet Yarra Valley Cabernet Sauvignon 2014

Yarra Valley

$30-$49

93/100

Firm and assertive, deeply ripened and long term; minty small berry flavour.

Giant Steps Primavera Vineyard Pinot Noir 2015

Yarra Valley

$50-$99

94/100

Dusty, floral and faintly herbal, with delicate cherry/berry fruit.

La Boheme Act Four Syrah Gamay 2015

Yarra Valley

$12-$19

90/100

Peppery, spicy and floral; smooth, mouthfiling and juicy.

Oakridge 864 Winery Block Syrah 2013

Yarra Valley

$50-$99

93/100

Elegant, dusty and perfumed, long and savoury, smooth and supple.

VICTORIA

Rob Dolan White Label Chardonnay 2015
Yarra Valley
$20-$29
93/100
Smooth and voluptuous, with generous peach, melon and grapefruit flavour.

Rochford La Gauche Cabernet Sauvignon 2015
Yarra Valley
$30-$49
92/100
Long and elegant, with pristine small dark berry fruit and cedary oak.

Soumah Wild Savagnin 2015
Yarra Valley
$30-$49
92/100
Pungent and smoky, floral and spicy, with luscious melon/apple flavour.

TarraWarra Estate Roussanne Marsanne Viognier 2015
Yarra Valley
$30-$49
92/100
Creamy, fragrant and savoury, with spicy tea tin, Turkish delight character.

Yeringberg Chardonnay 2015
Yarra Valley
$30-$49
96/100
Penetrative, pristine and highly complex, perfectly balanced and mouthwatering.

JEREMY'S PICK OF YARRA VALLEY CELLAR DOORS

NAME	ADDRESS	CONTACT	SPECIAL FACILITIES
De Bortoli Yarra Valley	58 Pinnacle Lane Dixon's Creek Vic 3775	(03) 5965 2271 www.debortoli.com.au	Choose from a variety of experiences that involve winery or vineyard tours or simply gourmet food and wine.
Giant Steps	336 Maroondah Highway Healesville Vic 3777	(03) 5962 6111 mail@giantsteps.com.au www.giantstepswine.com.au	Situated in the vibrant heart of Healesville, everything is on show at this cellar door. Taste wines in the barrel hall, where private dining is also available, or enjoy breakfast or lunch in the restaurant.
Levantine Hill	882 Maroondah Highway Coldstream Vic 3770	(03) 5962 1333 enquiry@levantinehill.com.au www.levantinehill.com.au	Stunning cellar door featuring barrel shaped tasting pods and a range of tasting experiences. Dine at Ezard@Levantine Hill for a spectacular gastronomic journey or stay in the Homestead for a true luxury experience.
Yering Station	38 Melba Highway Yarra Glen Vic 3775	(03) 9730 0100 info@yering.com www.yering.com	Victoria's first vineyard and original winery building built in the 1850s. Private wine and cheese tastings available, art gallery, produce store, monthly farmers' market and popular restaurant.

WESTERN AUSTRALIA

Given the relatively small size of its wine industry when compared to the eastern states, Western Australia produces a disproportionately large amount of Australia's finest wine. Its wine companies are more focused on the top end of the market than those of other states. Western Australia has a relatively small number of wine regions, but they are all distinctively different and clearly defined.

Great Southern

A very large, if sparsely populated wine region that encompasses some very fine smaller areas including Mount Barker, Denmark, the Porongorups and Frankland River. The coolest and most southerly of Western Australia's wine areas, its specialities are riesling, shiraz and cabernet sauvignon. Many of its wines are today made in a more European style.

Cherubino Great Southern Riesling 2015
Great Southern
$30-$49
95/100
Musky and perfumed, long and pristine, with a lingering core of piercing fruit.

Ferngrove King Malbec 2014
Frankland River
$20-$29
91/100
Sweetly oaked, with pastille-like red, black and blue fruits.

Frankland Estate Isolation Ridge Vineyard Riesling 2015
Frankland River
$30-$49
95/100
A waxy lemon blossom perfume, a luscious core of citrusy flavour and taut acids.

Houghton Crofters Cabernet Sauvignon 2014
Frankland River
$12-$19
94/100
Elegant, polished and shapley; pristine berry/cherry fruit and cedary oak.

Howard Park Scotsdale Shiraz 2014
Great Southern
$30-$49
92/100
Sweet red and black berries, peppery scents and meaty undertones.

JEREMY'S PICK OF GREAT SOUTHERN CELLAR DOORS

NAME	ADDRESS	CONTACT	SPECIAL FACILITIES
Castelli Estate	390 Mount Shadforth Road Denmark WA 6333	08 9848 3174 admin@castelligroup.com.au www.castelliestate.com.au	Bistro open 7 days for lunch and dinner; Castelli Lodge offers 5 quality bed and breakfast suites.
Rickety Gate	1949 Scotsdale Road Denmark WA 6333	08 9840 9503 wine@ricketygate.com.au ricketygateestate.com.au	Kirby's Restaurant features seasonal lunch menu on weekends, monthly dinners and cooking classes.
Singlefile	90 Walter Road Denmark WA 6333	08 9840 9749 thecellar@singlefilewines.com www.singlefilewines.com	Named for the resident family of geese who roam the property in single file. Wine and chocolate pairings, byo picnic.
Oranje Tractor Wine	198 Link Road Marbelup via Albany WA 6330	08 9842 5175 pam@oranjetractor.com www.oranjetractor.com	Wine flights offered every Sunday and personalised tastings and tours by appointment. Organic produce grown on the property and regular special events.

Margaret River

Perhaps the best of all Australian wine regions to visit, Margaret River has a maritime location adjacent to the Indian Ocean. It is home to several of Australia's finest and most powerful chardonnays, its most refined and classically stylish blends of cabernet sauvignon and merlot, and many of its most zesty, herbaceous and refreshing blends of semillon and sauvignon blanc. It's the powerhouse of Western Australian wine.

Cape Mentelle Zinfandel 2014

Margaret River

$50-$99

95/100

Deliciously smooth and vibrant, steeped in briary, confectionary fruit.

Deep Woods Estate Reserve Block 7 Shiraz 2014

Margaret River

$30-$49

92/100

Smooth and velvety, with translucent brambly fruit and mocha-like oak.

Evans & Tate Metricup Road Chardonnay 2015

Margaret River

$20-$29

92/100

Complex and savoury; grapefruit and melon, smoky

Houghton Gladstones Cabernet Sauvignon 2014

Margaret River

$50-$99

95/100

Long, fine-grained and artfully balanced; wonderful fruit

Leeuwin Estate Art Series Sauvignon Blanc 2015

Margaret River

$30-$49

93/100

Punchy and faintly herbal; juicy lychee fruit and restrained oak.

WESTERN AUSTRALIA

Peccavi Cabernet Sauvignon 2012

Margaret River

$30-$49

96/100

De luxe cabernet; deeply layered, long and complete. Superb.

Sandalford Estate Reserve Sauvignon Blanc Semillon 2015

Margaret River

$20-$29

92/100

Faintly tropical, intense and mouthwatering; finishing lemony and mineral.

Vasse Felix Heytesbury Chardonnay 2014

Margaret River

$50-$99

96/100

Pristine and translucently clear; mouthfilling and tightly focused.

Voyager Estate Sauvignon Blanc Semillon 2014

Margaret River

$20-$29

94/100

Penetrative and vivacious, with pristine fruit and delightfully fresh acids.

Woodlands Margaret Cabernet Blend 2014

Margaret River

$30-$49

95/100

Elegant and finely structured, long and pristine. Benchmark stuff.

JEREMY'S PICK OF MARGARET RIVER CELLAR DOORS

NAME	ADDRESS	CONTACT	SPECIAL FACILITIES
Leeuwin Estate	Stevens Road Margaret River WA 6285	(08) 9759 0000 info@leeuwinestate.com.au www.leeuwinestate.com.au	A true wine and food destination offering unique behind the scenes wine and food experiences. Leeuwin's famous restaurant and an art gallery featuring over 150 works.
Voyager Estate	Stevens Road Margaret River WA 6285	(08) 9757 6354 wineroom@voyagerestate.com.au www.voyagerestate.com.au	Exciting winery destination offering a comprehensive selection of tours, tasting experiences, stunning gardens and restaurant featuring two Wine Discovery menus.
Vasse Felix	Corner Caves Road & Tom Cullity Drive) Cowaramup WA 6284	(08) 9756 5000 info@vassefelix.com.au www.vassefelix.com.au	Margaret River's founding estate features an award winning restaurant, wine lounge, estate tours and art gallery showcasing a seasonal program of exhibitions.

WESTERN AUSTRALIA

Pemberton

A relatively youthful inland region towards the south of Western Australia, Pemberton (also known as Manjimup) is building a name for its fresh, tangy sauvignon blanc, refreshing chardonnay and finely balanced merlot. It's quite remote, but the trip is worth it!

Bellarmine Riesling Dry 2015

Pemberton

$20-$29

93/100

Fresh floral, apple and lemon zest aromas; long, penetrative and steely. Dry!

Bellarmine Shiraz 2010

Pemberton

$20-$29

92/100

Scented with tar, cola and blood plums; smoky and meaty, fiery and savoury.

Houghton Wisdom Sauvignon Blanc 2014

Pemberton

$20-$29

92/100

Punchy, fresh and faintly tropical, with tangy acids and a hint of nettle.

The Yard Channybearup Vineyard Sauvignon Blanc 2015

Pemberton

$20-$29

93/100

Luscious and creamy, with rich guava and lychee fruit and toasty, buttery oak.

JEREMY'S PICK OF PEMBERTON CELLAR DOORS

NAME	ADDRESS	CONTACT	SPECIAL FACILITIES
Silkwood Wines	9649 Channybearup Road Pemberton WA 6260	(08) 9776 1535 silkwood@ silkwoodwines.com.au www.silkwoodwines.com.au	Boutique winery property featuring lakeside restaurant and 5-star chalets with uninterrupted views of the lake and forest.
Smithbrook Wines	Smithbrook Road Pemberton WA 6260	08 9772 3557 stephenb@ fogartywines.com.au www.smithbrookwines.com.au	Bordered by towering Karri trees, this organically farmed vineyard property is also home to truffles and freshwater marron. Open by appointment only.
Lost Lake Wines	14591 Vasse Highway Pemberton WA 6260	(08) 9776 1251 info@lostlake.com.au www.lostlake.com.au	Strong believers in natural and organic farming, visitors may encounter the resident alpacas and guinea fowl. Restaurant and providore open Friday to Tuesday.

PAIRING WINE AND FOOD

An Easy Approach

Food and wine were made for each other. No other beverage offers anything like its diversity and complementary ability with food. Wherever wine is grown it has usually evolved hand in hand with the cuisine of its region. Indeed some wines actually need to be served with food to reveal their true quality and character.

Sure there are long-established so-called 'rules' of matching wine and food. The first thing most of us are told is to pair white wine with white meat and red wine with red meat. If everything we ate was boiled, there's perhaps the tiniest amount of sense in that advice. So let's forget it and start afresh.

Think about your choice of wine as an extension of the meal on the plate, and use a similar sort of logic when choosing it as you have already demonstrated when designing or ordering the actual meal itself.

Think about colours, textures, richness, intensity and flavours. When considering the colour of a meat – or even seafood – think also of how its preparation might have changed its nature, if at all. The dressing or sauce may equally contribute in a major way to the meal, and indeed the wine should perhaps be chosen with the dressing more in mind than the principal ingredient itself, especially if it becomes the dominant taste or texture.

Rule 1

It's important to match the intensity of flavour between the wine and the dish. A wine with a delicate flavour won't be noticed if paired with an intense dish, and the obverse also applies. So with a delicate steamed fish you don't serve a powerful oak-matured chardonnay; with a veal carpaccio you keep your bold shiraz in the cupboard.

CONTRAST OR COMPLEMENT?

There are two ways to get a result here, and the best results usually reflect a combination of the two. The object is to set off the food and the wine against each other by creating a difference that isn't too stark, but instead highlights their better qualities and differences. If the flavours or characteristics of food and wine are too similar, they just compete. For that reason, crisp, tart wines with highly acidic foods are out of the question – they clash. A certain contrast between the two helps to highlight the better qualities and individuality of both and shifts your attention from one to the other as you move through the meal.

Rule 2

Think about your choice of wine and dish from the angle of contrast/complement.

Here are some simple examples, just to get you thinking this way.

Let's say you're about to barbecue a whole flounder the old-fashioned way, with fresh lemon juice and butter. The taste of the fish is sweet but delicate, and in its cooking you're introducing the lemon and butter, each of which influence its ultimate taste. A delicate, relatively lean and crisp chardonnay, made with tightly-integrated oak will have similar flavour intensity. Its palate weight is also comparable – so here are the points that complement. Furthermore, the lemon juice will complement the acidity in the wine and also the lemon in its flavour profile. The acidity in the wine will help wrap up and freshen your palate after the fleshiness of the fish and the buttery, creamy taste you introduced at the barbecue.

Now let's pair a common dish involving red meat – roast lamb loin with a redcurrant and peppercorn sauce. At its best, this is a very intense dish, but a densely packed, treacle-like red wine would kill it off completely. So you're best to choose something medium to full in flavour. Similarly, its texture is of a fuller kind, but without being over the scale. Importantly, the sauce might indeed prove richer than the meat itself. So you complement the dish with a red of fuller body, without being excessively heavy or powerful. If made in a more elegant

style, whether from a warm or cooler climate, shiraz can reveal a strong peppery aspect as well as a taste of redcurrant. More complement – adding to the tightness and appropriateness of the match.

Some riper red wines, including a number made by Penfolds, often reveal a suggestion of roasting pan juices, which can provide another kind of flavour connection with roast red meat dishes.

Rule 3

Texture plays an obvious role. If the dish is stronger, meatier and richer than that just discussed, try a red with more firmness and tannin. The gravelly structures of firmer reds contrast with the fattiness or creaminess of richer sauces and dressings. If however, the dish is gentle and delicate, it could easily be smothered by such a wine.

Let's take this a step further. You might instead prefer to contrast texture and richness, rather than complement it. Thinking of dessert now, what might we pair with an old-fashioned trifle? On one hand you might choose a rich, luscious, profoundly sweet and deeply concentrated dessert wine that complements the trifle in just about every single way. But how much of the wine are you then actually going to drink? Might the combination be just too rich, too sweet and too overwhelming?

So, on the other hand, you might

choose to ease back with your choice of dessert wine, selecting instead a wine that is genuinely sweet but not tremendously so – registering perhaps as a 'spatlese' on a Germanic scale, or pretty much at the tame end of dessert wine sweetness. Such wines are not thick and gluggy, retain plenty of refreshing acidity and deliver bright, intense flavours without any heaviness. In this case, their texture and richness works well in a contrasting sense with the dessert.

If you take this approach at any stage throughout the meal, Rule 1 still applies – you need to match or complement the levels of flavour intensity between the wine and the dish.

Rule 4

Never stop experimenting with different combinations of wine and food.

Rule 5

If you like a combination of food and wine, it's a good match. Nobody else has the right to tell you it's not!

Popular

ALL WINE GOES WITH ALL CHEESE

It's a popular notion that any wine will go with any cheese. Strong, pungent cheeses like Stilton and Gippsland Blue absolutely steamroll delicate white wines. When pairing with wine, think about the fattiness, depth of flavour, texture and acidity of the cheese. For example, tannic wines may require drier, tarter cheeses, and creamy cheeses may demand an acidic wine.

At the corporate dinners I host, where I do my best to pair food and wine, I will often suggest a selection of cheeses paired with red wines before or instead of dessert. With red wines it makes little sense to serve popular choices like a runny soft-ripened cheese, a young, fresh, creamy goat or sheep's milk cheese or a pungent, deeply ripened washed rind. With red wines, especially those with age, I typically stipulate a drier, harder and more mature cheese like a Gruyere, a cloth-matured cheddar or a decent lump of reggiano. The texture, depth of flavour and acidity of these wines tends to marry best with the tannins, flavours and acids of dry red wines.

Here are some combinations of wine and cheese you might try:

- A full-bodied vintage red wine with a full-bodied vintage cheddar,
- A ripe camembert or brie with a dry riesling, fiano or a chardonnay,
- A mild, mellow gouda with a soft, perfumed pinot noir,
- The mild, salty taste of fetta with the minerality of a barrel-fermented

Misconceptions

sauvignon blanc-semillon blend,
- A mild, nutty edam with savagnin,
- A fruit cheese with a late-picked white style or muscat,
- A blue cheese with a late-harvest dessert wine,
- A frisky sauvignon blanc with a soft chevre.

YOU CAN'T MATCH WINE WITH CHINESE CUISINE

There's no doubt at all that with some dishes from cuisines such as Sichuan (Chuan) and Yunnan are more than challenging with wine thanks to the extreme presence of spice, chilli and the numbing effects of Sichuan pepper (hua jiao). That said, there's a wealth of incredible Chinese cuisine, much of which has yet to make its way to Australia, with which wine can match as perfectly as it does with any western cuisine.

To be general, with Chinese cuisine it's essential to consider what, exactly in the dish is contributing the most dominant flavours and textures. Might it be a delicate piece of seafood, or might it be a powerful combination of dried chilli and hua jiao? The preparation of or accompaniment to a meat, fowl or fish may have entirely changed its character so it might be smarter to choose a wine based on its dressing or sauce. An egg or a piece of tofu, might have been prepared and matured in such a way that it becomes emphatically pungent and powerful.

A typical braised meat dish might

have been prepared with a powerful presence of soy, sugar, hoisin sauce, ginger or spring onion, each of which impact strongly on its taste, and therefore the best choice of accompanying wine. Hoisin sauce typically needs some sweetness in a wine, either from the sweet oak in a rich chardonnay, perhaps, or from a slightly late-harvest white wine with residual sweetness.

Much of the Chinese food found in Australia is Cantonese (Yue) in style. While Australian Cantonese food is typically sweeter than found in mainland China and Hong Kong, it's perhaps the easiest of all Chinese cuisines to pair with wine. Yue cuisine is typically light and harmonious, featuring pork, crustaceans and shellfish, plus poultry and beef. It's easy to understand and, generally, doesn't contain too many surprises!

Fruit-focused white wines with racy acidity, such as riesling, the drier and more mineral sauvignon blancs and blends with semillon blends and the tauter, leaner chardonnays work perfectly with dim sum. Fuller whites, older even, can be paired with lobster, poultry and pork, although pinot noir can cross over here, depending on the sauce that might ultimately set the tone. Some of the more pungent seafood, dried abalone for instance, is more typically served with a firmish red whose tannins counter the texture of the dish. The more pepper and the richer the meat dish, the easier it becomes for red wines to pair nicely.

If you are preparing your own traditional Chinese dishes from provinces whose cuisines can be more confronting, perhaps ease back on some of the more challenging aspects, such as diced garlic or salty fermented beans. It will then be easier to marry your food with wine.

Western cuisine has evolved a sequence of serving food and wine that typically enables an order of wine service from an aperitif to dry whites, lighter and then fuller-bodied reds, then perhaps to a dessert or even fortified wine. This absolutely does not work if the intention is to serve Chinese cuisine in an order that is faithful to the origins and traditions of the cuisine itself. My view is to respect the cuisine by adapting the order that wine is presented. It makes the experience more authentic and perhaps more interesting and eye-opening for most western people.

Finally, it goes without saying that the way Chinese people typically share food around a large round table, with dish appearing after dish in an order than most western people would not instinctively understand, does make the precise matching of wine and food almost an impossibility when compared to the course-by-course sequence usually experienced at western tables.

There is however an easy solution: allocate three wine glasses per (adult) person, into which is poured, left to right, a leaner dry white, a fuller dry white (or soft red) and a firm dry red. Then you can enjoy the wine just as you enjoy the cuisine, mixing and matching along the way. All the pressure of creating the perfect match is immediately removed, and you're left to make new discoveries for your own palate.

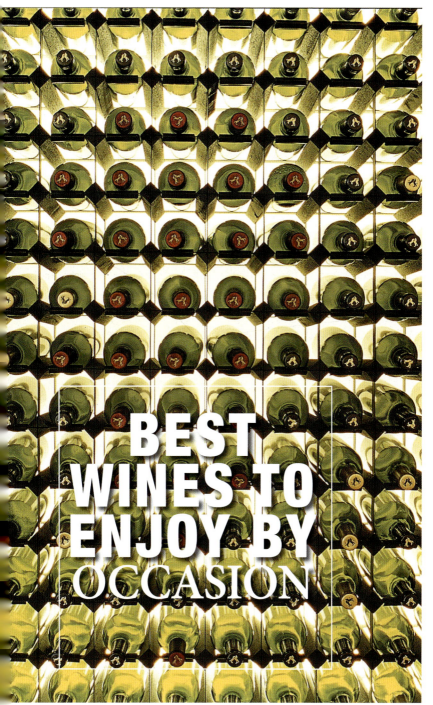

INFORMAL LUNCHTIME QUAFF

*J*ust the kind of fresh lively red, white and rosé you could enjoy over a glass or two before staging a return to the coalface...

Alta Sauvignon Blanc 2015

Adelaide Hills

$12-$19

92/100

Pristine passionfruit, gooseberry and cassis flavour wrapped in fresh acids.

Castle Rock Estate Diletti Chardonnay 2015

Porongorup

$20-$29

91/100

Fresh peach, lemon and grapefruit with nutty, creamy undertones.

Capercaillie The Clan Cabernet Blend 2014

Barossa Valle, Lower Hunter Valley

$30-$49

90/100

Bright, fresh and sweetly fruited; then more saovury and herbal at the finish.

Henschke Louis Semillon 2014

Eden Valley

$20-$29

93/100

Tobaccoey honeydew melon fruit backed by faintly smoky vanilla oak.

Lerida Estate Cullerin Pinot Noir 2014

Canberra

$30-$49

91/100

Mouthfilling spicy red cherry/berry fruit with earth undertones.

**Montara
Old
Bush
Pinot Noir
2014**

Grampians

$20-$29

/100

...sty, earthy
and floral; long,
...ppy and
...voury.

**Oakridge
Willowlake
Vineyard
Sauvignon
2014**

Yarra Valley

$30-$49

94/100

Complex and
waxy with a
luscious core
of gooseberry
and lychees.

**Peccavi
No Regrets
Sauvignon
Blanc
Semillon
2015**

Margaret River

$20-$29

92/100

Vivacious fruit
backed by a
hint of oak and
nutty, creamy
complexity.

**Riposte The
Stiletto Pinot
Gris 2015**

Adelaide Hills

$20-$29

90/100

Smooth and
creamy, with
tranlucent
pear/apple
flavour.

**SC Pannell
Tempranillo
Touriga
2014**

McLaren Vale,
Barossa Valley

$20-$29

92/100

Medium-
bodied, floral
and spicy with
juicy dark
berry fruit.

CHILLING ON AN AFTERNOON

Pure indulgence but also rather more cerebral, since you have the time to think as you drink. So here are some slightly sweet or evolving whites and medium bodied, savoury reds.

Bindi Block 5 Pinot Noir 2015
Macedon Ranges
$50-$99
96/100
Waiting to build; supremely floral, intense and elegant.

Briar Ridge Dairy Hill Shiraz 2014
Lower Hunter Valley
$50-$99
93/100
Spicy, peppery and floral; long and smoky with sour-edged fruit.

Frankland Estate Smith Cullam Riesling 2015
Frankland River
$50-$99
95/100
Scented with apple blossom and potpourri, long and marginally sweet.

Hardys Eileen Hardy Pinot Noir 2014
Tasmania
$50-$99
96/100
Heady, wild and meaty; long and smooth; densely packed with pristine fruit.

HEWITSON Old Garden BAROSSA VALLEY Mourvèdre

Hewitson Old Garden Mourvèdre 2013
Barossa Valley
$100-$199
95/100
Deeply floral, restrained and velvety, smooth and elegant.

**cPherson
WC Shiraz
ourvedre
014**

ctoria

20-$29

/100

eppery and
avoury, with
tense dark
erries backed
y charcuterie
tes.

**Moorilla
Muse Series
Methode
Traditionelle
Extra Brut
Rosé 2009**

Tasmania

$50-$99

94/100

Wild fruits, game meats and undertones of brioche, taut and savoury.

**Oakridge 864
Drive Block
Chardonnay
2014**

Yarra Valley

$50-$99

95/100

Racy, taut and briny, with pristine stonefruit, grapefruit and lemon blossom notes.

**Rochford
Yarra Valley
Cerberus 2015**

Yarra Valley

$20-$29

92/100

Musky, floral and savoury; long and juicy, finishing long and savoury.

**Rockford
Hand Picked
Riesling 2013**

Eden Valley

$30-$49

93/100

Toasty and buttery, with sumptuous lemon/lime flavour and fresh acids.

BRING ON THE BARBECUE!

Sure they're ripe and flavoursome, with some genuine texture that could be quite firm on occasions, but just because you're having a barbecue doesn't mean you shouldn't enjoy a decent red!

All Saints Estate Shiraz 2014
Rutherglen
$20-$29
91/100
Lively dark fruits, fresh vanilla oak, with notes of licorice and white pepper.

Bremerton Old Adam Shiraz 2013
Langhorne Creek
$50-$99
92/100
Sumptuously ripened, richly oaked, bold and handsomely balanced.

Cullen Mangan Red Blend 2015
Margaret River
$20-$29
94/100
Profoundly floral; dark plums and cherries; fine, crunchy tannins.

d'Arenberg The Ironstone Pressings Grenache Shiraz Mourvèdre Blend 2012
McLaren Vale
$50-$99
94/100
Meaty, dark-fruited and firmish, with deep, brooding flavour.

Dalwhinnie Southwest Rocks Shiraz 2012
Pyrenees
$50-$99
93/100
Long, dark and savoury; firmish but gentle; lingering note of licorice.

Fox Creek Reserve Shiraz 2014

McLaren Vale

$50-$99

99/100

Sumptuous and polished with lavish dark fruits, velvet tannins and meaty complexity.

Langmeil Three Gardens Shiraz Grenache Mourvèdre Blend 2013

Barossa Valley

$20-$29

92/100

Generous, soft and seamless; luscious blue fruits; fine gravelly tannins.

Mr Riggs Shiraz 2013

McLaren Vale

$50-$99

95/100

Firm and vibrant, with deep layers of pristine small fruits and tight-grained oak.

Passing Clouds The Angel Cabernet Blend 2014

Bendigo

$30-$49

92/100

Floral and cedary, long and smooth, with a vibrant core of fruit.

Peter Lehmann Futures Shiraz 2013

Barossa Valley

$20-$29

93/100

Dark-fruited, polished and densely packed; long and mineral.

SUNSET SENSATIONS

Sunset demands refreshing and exotic, so here's a list of pure and vivacious white and sparkling wines that explode with personality and character.

Alkoomi Riesling 2015
Frankland River
$20-$29
94/100
Punchy, floral and spicy, with intense lime, lemon and apple flavours, tangy acids,

Bindi Kostas Rind Chardonnay 2015
Macedon Ranges
$30-$49
95/100
Citrus, floral and mineral aromas; long and translucent, smoked meat finish.

Castagna Ingenue Viognier 2014
Beechworth
$50-$99
95/100
Spicy and musky, apricot kernels and minerals, luscious and juicy.

Castle Rock Estate A & W Reserve Riesling 2016
Porongorup
$20-$29
93/100
Musk, guava and tea tin aromas, long and bright, with tangy lime

Clonakilla Viognier 2015
Canberra
$30-$49
92/100
Scented with honeysuckle, apricot and minerals; long, restrained and savoury.

**urly Flat
he Curly
hardonnay
·13**

acedon
anges

0-$99

/100

edium to
-bodied,
grant and
eamy,
nslucently
ght and
sh.

**Leasingham
Classic Clare
Riesling 2009**

Clare Valley

$30-$49

95/100

Toasty and
waxy, taut and
sculpted, long
and citrusy, oily
and buttery.

**Mount Mary
Triolet 2014**

Yarra Valley

$50-$99

95/100

Floral and
smoky;
fresh melon,
lemon and
gooseberries;

**Seppelt
Drumborg
Vineyard
Chardonnay
2014**

Henty

$30-$49

96/100

Complex,
floral and
creamy; gentle
and crystalline;
finishes
savoury.

**Yarrabank
Cuvée
Sparkling
2011**

Victoria

$30-$49

93/100

Pristine, toasty
and citrusy;
long and
chalky; crunchy
and mineral.

WEEKNIGHTS AT HOME

ust because you're staying home during the week, it doesn't mean you shouldn't drink well. There are, after all, only so many more wines you will enjoy in this lifetime! But you don't need to spend a fortune…!

Best's Great Western Bin No. 1 Shiraz 2015

Grampians Great Western

$20-$29

91/100

Cracked pepper and herbs, blackcurrants and mulberries, gentle and dusty.

Castle Rock Estate Porongorup Sauvignon Blanc 2016

Porongorup

$20-$29

91/100

Vibrant and pristine, with juicy passionfruit, gooseberries and lychees.

Coriole Cabernet Sauvignon 2014

McLaren Vale

$20-$29

93/100

Elegant, perfumed and medium-bodied; luscious pastille fruit.

d'Arenberg The Custodian Grenache 2013

McLaren Vale

$20-$29

91/100

Baked earth, blueberries and rhubarb; rustic, firm and mouthfilling.

Fox Creek Short Row Shiraz 2014

McLaren Vale

$20-$29

93/100

Fine-grained, elegant and juicy, with dark fruits and chocolate flavours.

**Jappstein
kland
eyard
sling 2015**

are Valley

$20-$29

/100

stine and
rfumed, taut
d refreshing,
e and racy.

Mountainside Shiraz 2015

Grampians

$20-$29

92/100

Musky, floral and peppery; medium in weight, long and savoury.

Redman Shiraz 2014

Coonawarra

$20-$29

92/100

Long, gentle and evenly paced; savoury and supple.

Vasse Felix Filius Cabernet Sauvignon 2014

Margaret River

$20-$29

90/100

Sweet plum/mulberry fruit, cedar/vanilla oak; gentle and fine-grained.

Yering Station Yarra Valley Chardonnay 2013

Yarra Valley

$20-$29

94/100

Smoky and mineral, with bright stonefruits and citrus, brisk acids.

PARTY, PARTY!

*T*here's no need to blow the budget here – so here's a list of delicious, inexpensive crowd pleasers covering fizz, whites and reds.

Ferngrove Frankland River Sauvignon Blanc 2015
Frankland River
$12-$19
89/100
Punchy and mouthfilling, with bright tropical and lychee flavours, limey acids..

Hardys Sir James Vintage Pinot Noir Chardonnay 2009
Various
$20-$29
89/100
Rich and creamy, with deep stonefruit, tropical and smoked meat flavours.

Jim Barry The Lodge Hill Shiraz 2014
Clare Valley
$20-$29
90/100
Medium to full-bodied; laced with minty, juicy small berries and cherries.

John Duval Plexus Shiraz Grenache Mourvèdre Blend 2014
Barossa Valley
$20-$29
92/100
Luscious and velvety, with briary small fruits, licorice notes.

Millbrook Petit Verdot 2014
Perth Hills
$20-$29
91/100
Pastille-like plums and berries over notes of cola, rhubarb and dried herbs.

**itchell
ataro
enache
12**

are Valley

0-$29

/100

edium-
died, smooth
d soft; earthy
d rustic, wild
d briary.

Peccavi No Regrets Cabernet Merlot 2014

Margaret River

$20-$29

92/100

Fragrant and brightly lit, long and juicy, with fine-honed tannins and style.

Red Claw Chardonnay 2015

Mornington Peninsula

$20-$29

90/100

Fruit-focused, with bright peach, pear and green apple flavours, brisk acids.

Seppelt Chalambar Shiraz 2014

Grampians, Heathcote

$20-$29

93/100

Elegant, luscious, dark-fruited and sour-edged; superb elegance and value.

Stella Bella Cabernet Merlot 2015

Margaret River

$20-$29

91/100

Sweet small berries and cherries backed by creamy oak and tobacco.

DOING IT FORMAL

Ok, here's what you choose if you're after something a little more swanky, pricey and showy. None of these will let you down!

Brown Brothers Patricia Noble Riesling 2013

King Valley

$30-$49

95/100

Candied citrus and creme brulée; long and luscious; balanced finish.

Mitolo Reiver Shiraz 2013

Barossa Valley

$50-$99

94/100

Luxuriant dark fruit, handsome oak; long, firm and faintly mineral.

Moorilla Muse Series Methode Traditionelle Extra Brut 2010

Tasmania

$50-$99

94/100

Complex, floral rosé with crackly bakery yeast influences; savoury.

Primo Estate Joseph Angel Gully Shiraz 2014

Clarendon

$50-$99

94/100

Dense dark fruits, smoky mocha/chocolate oak, licorice finish.

Rochford Premier Pinot Noir 2015

Yarra Valley

$50-$99

96/100

Musky Morello cherries, plums and cola; concentrated and mouthfilling.

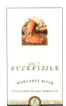

Lane Vineyard, The RG Chardonnay 2012

Adelaide Hills

$100-$199

95/100

Lavish stonefruit and grapefruit, cloves and ginger, long and savoury.

Suckfizzle Margaret River Sauvignon Blanc Semillon 2012

Margaret River

$30-$49

95/100

Smoky citrus and melon, nougat and creamy oak; long and briny.

Tomboy Hill The Tomboy Pinot Noir 2014

Ballarat

$50-$99

94/100

Musky, floral and spicy, with pristine cherry/berry fruit and fine tannins.

Torbreck Les Amis Grenache 2013

Barossa Valley

$100-$199

93/100

Assertive, concentrated and densely packed; earthy and smoky.

Yalumba The Octavius Shiraz 2012

Barossa Valley

$100-$199

97/100

Remarkable depth, polish and balance; pristine berry plum fruit and great oak.

WINDING DOWN

So now you want something more thoughtful and interesting, without being hammered by excessive fruitiness, alcohol or oak. Here's a list of maturing whites and fascinating reds that you can kick back with.

All Saints Estate Family Cellar Marsanne 2013

Rutherglen

$30-$49

92/100

Toasty lemon butter and honeysuckle; chewy, savoury and smoky.

Charles Melton Grains of Paradise Shiraz 2013

Barossa Valley

$50-$99

93/100

Gamey dark berries and blood plums; long, smooth and sour-edged.

Freeman Secco Rondinella Corvina 2012

Hilltops

$30-$49

94/100

Dusty and herbal, long and polished; meaty presence of dark berries, citrus.

Freycinet Cabernet Merlot 2013

East Coast Tasmania

$30-$49

96/100

Cigarboxy, floral and dark fruit aromas; long, fine-grained and stylish.

McAlister Vineyards The McAlister 2009

Gippsland

$50-$99

92/100

Wild, gravelly, mineral and savoury; charmingly complex and rustic.

Rockford Local Growers Semillon 2013

Barossa Valley

$20-$29

93/100

Swinney Tirra Lirra Cabernet Sauvignon Tempranillo Grenache 2014

Frankland River

$30-$49

91/100

Assertive, with sour-edged dark berries, chocolatey oak; long and firmish.

Tahbilk 1927 Vines Marsanne 2008

Nagambie Lakes

$30-$49

94/100

Creamy and nutty, with smoky, lanolin and honeysuckle notes, lemony

Tyrrell's Single Vineyard Stevens Semillon 2011

Lower Hunter Valley

$30-$49

94/100

Classically toasty and smoky, with lemon curd, green olives and minerals.

YarraLoch Stephanie's Dream Cabernet Sauvignon 2012

Yarra Valley

$30-$49

95/100

Superbly structured, smooth and fine-grained; vibrant fruit and finish.

THE JEREMY OLIVER WINE AWARDS:

The Benchmarks

Bass Phillip Reserve Pinot Noir 2014

South Gippsland

$200-$499

98/100

Astonishingly intense, complex and elegant; one of the truly great pinots.

Cloudburst Chardonnay 2015

Margaret River

$200-$499

97/100

Extraordinarily pure and powerful; effortlessly long and smooth, mineral finish.

Coldstream Hills Reserve Chardonnay 2014

Yarra Valley

$50-$99

97/100

Long-term, suave and complex; powerful and artfully balanced.

Coriole Lloyd Reserve Shiraz 2013

McLaren Vale

$50-$99

97/100

Supremely generous, fiery and impactful, but harmonious in all respects.

Giaconda Chardonnay 2014

Beechworth

$100-$199

98/100

Long and luscious, creamy and complex; lingering fruit, spice and struck match.

THE BEST BUYS IN 2017

TOP 10

Here's Jeremy Oliver's Top 10 for 2017. Jeremy is perhaps the toughest marker in Australia when it comes to allocating scores out of 100, but these are all **rated at 97 or above**. They're the style and quality leaders in Australia today.

Giaconda Estate Shiraz 2014

Beechworth

$100-$199

97/100

Outrageously complex, deep and savoury; layers of depth and texture.

House of Arras 20th Anniversary Late Disgorged 1998

Tasmania

$200-$499

97/100

Smoke, brioche and meaty notes; powerful, long and savoury. De luxe.

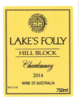

Lake's Folly Hill Block Chardonnay 2015

Lower Hunter Valley

$50-$99

97/100

Hugely complex, with superb melon/peach fruit and ham hock notes. Mineral.

Paradise IV Dardel Shiraz 2015

Geelong

$50-$99

98/100

Amazingly perfumed, densely packed with flavour, yet elegant and savoury.

Penfolds Grange Shiraz 2012

Barossa Valley, McLaren Vale

$500+

97/100

Steeped in fruit, handsomely augmented with oak and tannin – benchmark Grange.

THE JEREMY OLIVER WINE AWARDS:

The Affordable Classics

Best's Great Western Cabernet Sauvignon 2014

Grampians Great Western

$20-$29

93/100

Medium-bodied, polished and elegant; bright berry/plum flavour, pliant tannins.

Coriole Shiraz 2014

McLaren Vale

$20-$29

93/100

Elegant and peppery, with pristine small black and red berries, chocolate oak.

Ferngrove Majestic Cabernet Sauvignon 2014

Frankland River

$20-$29

92/100

Firm and drying, with fiery, earthy dark fruits and creamy oak.

Henschke Green's Hill Riesling 2015

Lenswood

$20-$29

94/100

Pristine floral lime and green apple skin aromas; long, focused and chalky.

Kilikanoon Mort's Block Riesling 2015

Clare Valley

$20-$29

94/100

Austere and penetrative; pristine lime/white peach flavour, lemony acids.

THE BEST BUYS IN 2017

under $30

Proof positive that we're still living in the Lucky Country! Here's a list of wonderful wines that shouldn't set you back a cent more than **$30**!

Montara Gold Rush Shiraz 2013
Grampians
$20-$29
93/100
Fragrant, meaty and spicy; berries, plums and fine crunchy tannins.

Passing Clouds Graeme's Shiraz Cabernet Blend 2015
Bendigo
$20-$29
93/100
Smooth, harmonious and luscious; peppery fruit knit with cedary oak.

Pewsey Vale Vineyard The Contours Riesling 2011
Eden Valley
$20-$29
95/100
Taut and racy; lemon tart and butter, toast and kerosene.

Tim Adams Shiraz 2013
Clare Valley
$20-$29
93/100
Minty dark berries, mocha oak and firmish tannins; long and palate-staining.

YarraLoch La Cosette Chardonnay 2014
Yarra Valley
$20-$29
95/100
Improbably great value – deeply ripened, complex and savoury.

THE JEREMY OLIVER WINE AWARDS:

Brilliant Budget Drops

Bleasdale Bremerview Shiraz 2014

Langhorne Creek

$12-$19

92/100

Bright mulberry/dark plum flavour; creamy cedary oak; cracked pepper.

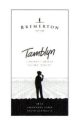

Bremerton Tamblyn Cabernet Blend 2013

Langhorne Creek

$12-$19

87/100

Jammy plum/ blackberry flavour, chocolate oak, drying and medium-bodied.

d'Arenberg The High Trellis Cabernet Sauvignon 2013

McLaren Vale

$12-$19

92/100

Profoundly floral and earthy; palate-staining dark fruit, firm and mineral.

Ferngrove Frankland River Merlot 2014

Frankland River

$12-$19

86/100

Medium-bodied, sweetly fruited, with chocolatey oak and marzipan.

Innocent Bystander Chardonnay 2014

Yarra Valley

$12-$19

91/100

Fragrant and spicy, with juicy peach and citrus flavours.

THE BEST BUYS IN 2017

Great cheapos

Ok, you're on a budget – it's not a problem. You can buy really good wine for **less than $20**, even **less than $10**! Here's a list to start with.

Jacob's Creek Reserve Chardonnay 2015
Adelaide Hills
$12-$19
90/100
Spotless and pure; vibrant and chalky with citrusy fruit.

Mount Langi Ghiran Billi Billi Shiraz 2013
Victoria
$12-$19
88/100
Peppery and chocolatey, with juicy dark berries, menthol and chalky tannin.

Oxford Landing Cabernet Sauvignon Shiraz 2014
South Australia
$5-$11
87/100
Pastille-like blackcurrants and red berries, vanilla oak and dusty tannins.

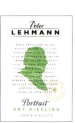

Peter Lehmann Barossa Portrait Riesling 2015
Eden Valley
$12-$19
92/100
Delicate lavender/lime juice perfume; long and lemony, dusty texture.

Primo Estate La Biondina Colombard 2016
Adelaide
$12-$19
88/100
Luscious and marginally sweet, with bright tropical, peach and apricot flavour.

THE JEREMY OLIVER WINE AWARDS:

Great wines to cellar

Bindi Quartz Chardonnay 2015

Macedon Ranges

$50-$99

96/100

Fragant and citrusy, with crystalline fruit and taut, tangy acids.

d'Arenberg The Dead Arm Shiraz 2012

McLaren Vale

$50-$99

95/100

Penetrative and mineral, with musky cracked pepper notes and spicy perfume.

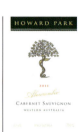

Howard Park Abercrombie Cabernet Sauvignon 2013

Mount Barke, Margaret River

$100-$199

95/100

Sweetly floral, vibrant and faintly herbal; long-term and gravelly.

Jacob's Creek Limited Edition Shiraz Cabernet 2010

Barossa Valley, Coonawarra

$100-$199

96/100

Sumptuous, polished and firm; lustrous fruit and tight-knit oak.

John Duval Eligo Shiraz 2013

Barossa Valley

$100-$199

95/100

Finely crafted, steeped in small dark fruits; soaks up new chocolatey oak.

THE BEST BUYS IN 2017

The classics

So you're after something classic to put into the cellar – for more than just a handful of years? Here's a list of currently available **long-term classics** that you can buy and cellar with complete confidence, provided of course you have the right conditions!

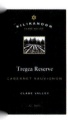

Kilikanoon Tregea Reserve Cabernet Sauvignon 2012
Clare Valley
$50-$99
95/100
Minty and herbal, with classical long-term depth, elegance and sinewy spine.

Penfolds Bin 707 Cabernet Sauvignon 2014
Barossa Valle, Padthawa, Port Lincoln
$200-$499
96/100
Deeply ripened but retains elegance; layers of fruit and drying structure.

Rockford Basket Press Shiraz 2012
Barossa Valley
$50-$99
96/100
Remarkably elegant, musky and spicy; becoming leathery; layered fruit.

Taylors St Andrews Riesling 2015
Clare Valley
$30-$49
95/100
Profoundly floral; pristine lime juice flavour; generous taut and frisky.

Yalumba The Menzies Cabernet Sauvignon 2013
Coonawarra
$50-$99
95/100
Dusty, floral and cigarboxy; long and elegant, firmish and balanced.

THE JEREMY OLIVER WINE AWARDS:

Jeremy's Must-Have...

Bowen Estate Cabernet Sauvignon 2014

Coonawarra

$30-$49

96/100

Brilliant long-term red; superbly structured, measured and balanced.

Cobaw Ridge Lagrein 2013

Macedon Ranges

$50-$99

95/100

Wild, briary and chocolatey, layered sour fruit and tannins, great acids.

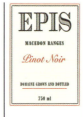

Epis Pinot Noir 2014

Macedon Ranges

$50-$99

96/100

Pristine, musky and floral; lustrous fruit; great length and structure.

Hewitson Private Cellar Falkenberg Vineyard Shiraz 2013

Barossa Valley

$50-$99

95/100

Seamlessly long, powerfully flavoured, yet soft and gentle; meaty evolution.

Houghton Jack Mann Cabernet Blend 2013

Frankland River

$100-$199

96/100

Classically structured, dark and cigarboxy, elegant and complex.

THE BEST BUYS IN 2017

MUST HAVES

It's now **pure indulgence** time for me. Here are the wines I'd just like to settle down with and enjoy – over a meal, a conversation or a good book. They're the kind of wines I'd never share with more than two people!

 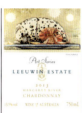  

Kilikanoon Mort's Reserve Riesling 2015

Clare Valley

$30-$49

96/100

Lavender and apple blossom perfume, mouthfilling and tightly focused; chalky.

Leeuwin Estate Art Series Chardonnay 2013

Margaret River

$50-$99

97/100

Impactful but fine and silky, with pure penetrative fruit, funkiness and brine.

Paradise IV Chaumont Cabernet Shiraz Blend 2015

Geelong

$50-$99

95/100

Wild and savoury, smoky and meaty; medium weight, long and pristine.

St Hugo Cabernet Shiraz 2013

Coonawarra, Barossa Valley

$50-$99

95/100

Penetrative and energetic; bloody fruit, cedary oak and firm tannins.

Wynns Coonawarra Estate V & A Lane Cabernet Shiraz 2014

Coonawarra

$30-$49

94/100

Meaty and peppery, with restrained fruit, dusty tannins and mouthwatering acids.

HOW WINE IS GROWN AND MADE

GROWING GRAPES

GOOD WINE NEEDS GOOD FRUIT

To make quality wine, fruit must be healthy and free from unwanted disease, well ripened and show the potential to suit the style of wine the maker is after. As grapes enter their final period of ripening, they accumulate sugar which is formed in the vine leaves through the process of photosynthesis and translocated into the grapes themselves. This is the sugar that is then fermented in the vinification process, producing the alcohol we find in finished wine. Grapes are typically harvested once their sugar content enables them to make a dry wine of between eleven and fifteen percent alcohol by volume. Other key factors in determining ripeness other than sugar content are the levels of flavour and acidity present in the grapes at harvest – as well as the ripeness of skins and seeds with red wines.

HOW CLIMATE AFFECTS WINE

Broadly speaking, cooler wine regions produce more restrained and finer-structured wines that can deliver very intense flavours from fruit that is harvested with naturally high levels of acidity. A cool climate firstly retards the ripening of the berry, then allows it to finish ripening after the summer's heat has passed, in the less-searing months of autumn. In Australia, some Victorian and Tasmanian vineyards can harvest as late as May, and

April picking is still a common sight in the southernmost wine regions of the country.

The period between budburst and flowering in the spring is sensitive to temperature and is retarded by cool climates. This pushes the whole ripening phase back later into the year, into the cooler autumn months – which has a profound effect on the fruit composition and is directly responsible for the 'cool climate' character of more intense fruit flavours and higher levels of natural acidity. Fruit from cooler climates is able to retain more of their delicate grape flavours than would be experienced if the same vine grew and ripened fruit in a warmer location.

Furthermore, the higher level of natural acidity found in cool-climate wine can be attributed to the rate at which the malic acid that naturally occurs in grapes is converted to tartaric acid (a softer acid) in the later stages of ripening. This process is temperature-driven and therefore occurs to a more significant extent in warmer areas, lowering the impact of the acidity of the natural grape acids.

Warm climate vineyards are frequently harvested in the heat of high summer, which is when much of their ripening and flavour development occurs. Warm climate wines are typically richer, rounder and broader. They are usually more impactful and mouthfilling than fruit from cooler climates and, as mentioned above, carry less natural acidity. In Australia wineries can add to their juice and wine the same acids that naturally evolve in grapes themselves. As you might expect, there is more acid adjustment in warmer regions.

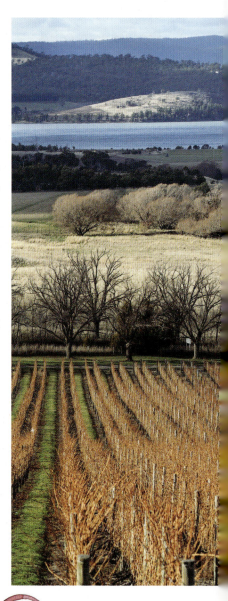

SOME VINEYARDS ARE BETTER THAN OTHERS

As you will see today, winemakers are going out of their way to focus on individual vineyard wines – wines that could only come from one particular place. However, it's only the very good or very poor sites that are able to really influence the taste of their wine.

Most of the world's very best wines do indeed reflect the geological and geographical situations of their site. Let me introduce a French term with a universal application: terroir. Terroir can be paraphrased as the ability of a wine to reflect such defining and distinctive elements such as the aspect, soil and microclimate of its vineyard. Where this applies, regardless of in which country or region they are grown, if the grapes are grown and harvested in a way that enables them to reflect the terroir of their vineyard, then that terroir will ultimately become the single most important factor as that wine ages, almost regardless of how the winemaker might actually make the wine.

To enable the terroir effect to shine through usually requires a relatively low cropping level of fruit, considerable attention to detail in the vineyard and the cellar, as well as the making of wines without faults.

However, the relationships between soils and wine is a less direct process. Some of the world's best vineyards are located in perhaps in a surprisingly wide variety of situations. In Champagne (France) they are found on solid chalk, in the Mosel (Germany) on slate cliffs and at Chateauneuf-du-Pape in the southern Rhône Valley (France) on plains covered by hefty boulders. Typically in Europe vines are planted close together, are not irrigated and experience some struggle or stress to fully ripen their crops.

Australia's best vineyards operate with similar levels of competition or stress. We have the oldest and typically least fertile soils in the world, some of which are planted to some of the country's most famous vineyards. Mean, infertile soils and a minimal application of irrigation water create substantial levels of stress in old, mature shiraz vineyards throughout South Australia and Victoria. Aside from some very recent warmer seasons, the cooler regions in Australia's southeast and in the far south of Western Australia are more than cold enough and late enough to challenge their vines

Wherever grapes are grown, the fundamental issues are precisely the same. Is the site good enough? Has the vineyard been set up to fully exploit the benefits of the site? Are the vines being tended in the best and most appropriate way to reflect the site's terroir? If the answers to all these questions is 'yes', there is a very good chance that the vineyard might produce very good wine, and wine that is noticeably distinct from that grown and made in virtually identical fashion from a neighbouring site, with just minor differences in soil, aspect and climate.

SEASONS AND VINTAGES ARE ANYTHING BUT EQUAL

Wine labels don't display a vintage year just to show how old they are, but also to give more than a hint as to their quality. Different years really do vary by an enormous amount, which is substantially reflected in the differences between their wines. It doesn't matter if the fruit was grown and the wine made in exactly the same manner.

Seasonal quality can be affected by a huge number of factors including frosts that kill crops partially or completely, fires and heatwaves, droughts or floods, pests or diseases. In the bottle this causes some vintages to take longer to reach maturity, or others to age more quickly. Remember, it's typically the best vineyard sites that typically are more reliable in the more challenging vintages. That's why they are the best and probably more expensive.

SUSTAINABLE VITICULTURE

Following the global trend towards organically produced food, there is also a strong trend in international wine to grow grapes with a minimal use of agricultural chemicals, if indeed they are used at all.

Twenty-five years ago, very few grape growers were genuinely interested in the health of their soils. If a site's soil lacked an important nutrient, you simply sprayed that

ORGANIC AND BIODYNAMIC

Many vineyards have adapted their techniques sufficiently to be certified as 'organic'. Many vineyards are nurtured to increase the diversity of their plant life with cover crops between vine rows, while steps are taken to increase the nutrient level and biological activity of their soils. Natural processes are implemented to develop a sustainable management system with natural solutions for nutrient cycling and pest, disease and weed management. Most organic standards typically allow the use of a limited range of acceptable chemicals such as fertilisers and pesticides.

Some growers have adopted a genuinely biodynamic approach, using special composts and other preparations according to a pre-determined calendar. Following the approach of its founder, Rudolf Steiner, biodynamics is an approach that considers the vineyard in its entirety as a living system within a wider pattern of lunar and cosmic rhythms. Whether or not we believe in the philosophies beneath it, it is hard not to acknowledge the positive contribution of biodynamics with respect to vineyard and vine health.

A large number of growers around the world use the tags 'organic' and 'biodynamic' to sell their wine. In my view the most important factors are the reduction in the use of vineyard chemicals and a sustainable approach to viticulture, whatever it is called. Winegrowers the world over have learned how important it is to respect their land and to ensure its vitality. Families, in particular, understand their custodial link with the lands they occupy and farm.

nutrient onto the vine directly. Soils were sterilised, flattened hard and in many parts of the world, considered largely irrelevant! It's hard to imagine such an approach today.

Many growers, in Australia and other wine-producing countries, are reducing or eliminating their use of fungicides, insecticides, herbicides and fertilizers in favour of a more organic approach. The upside is healthier soil, healthier vines and that are better-equipped to look after themselves if faced by difficult weather or the invasion of a pest or disease.

MAKING WINE

STARTING WITH JUICE

The first wine ever made was probably a sheer fluke - possibly a goatskin of grape juice left alone in the sun thousands of years ago. Perhaps the first hangover occurred about three-and-a-half hours later! Since then, modern winemaking has evolved to become equal parts art and science.

Step one is to crush the grapes into a mushy sort of medium called must, from the Ancient Greek for unfermented grape juice - 'mustum'. While the juice from nearly all grape varieties is colourless, red wines are given their colour by being left it in contact with the skins, which contain natural red pigments. To achieve deep, long-living colour, the juice for red wines is generally left in contact with the skins for much or all of the fermentation, which may last several days.

Winemakers choose how much of the grape skins and grape solids are allowed to remain in the must, depending on what sort of wine is being fermented. Only a few hours of skin contact if at all, to make a richer and more textural wine, are used for whites. A more textured and powerful chardonnay, for example, is typically made with more solid than a taut, racy riesling.

With white wine the juice is separated from the grapes prior to fermentation, the clearest and most intense of which, running freely from the skins is called 'free run'. The remaining skins and seeds are pressed to extract the juice that remains bound up in the flesh of the fruit. This 'pressings' juice is often kept aside from the free run. It is usually more bitter, coloured and lacks the delicacy and freshness of free run, but occasionally has more grunt and genuine varietal flavour. Some pressings may be added to the free run after fermentation to generate more body and complexity.

OF YEAST AND FERMENTATION

The juice is then 'seeded' to begin fermentation, often by adding pedigree yeasts, bred especially for the important job at hand: to convert the grape sugar to alcohol. Left to themselves, an industrious strain of yeast will convert all the grape sugar, leaving a very 'dry' wine - that is, entirely without any sweetness. You can stop the fermentation while some sugar still remains, leaving a sweet wine, by killing or removing the yeast. Macabre, but effective. They would die anyway, as they are actually killed by the alcohol they themselves produce.

Many winemakers opt for 'indigenous' or 'wild' yeasts for the fermentation. In most cases, this more diverse and native population comprises those yeasts that have come to inhabit the vineyard and winery over the years. Some might indeed be genuinely 'wild' or 'local', but where winemaking has occurred for a decade or more, this population is likely also to include genuine winemaking yeasts. 'Natural' ferments with these yeasts can help create wines of more complexity and character, but they can also be less reliable, producing undesirable smells and failing to finish the fermentation. It is best to wait until a winery has been used for winemaking for at least a decade before taking the risk and leaving wild yeasts to do the entire job.

REDS ARE DIFFERENT INDEED

It's fairly self-evident that red wines have more colour and texture than whites. They're fermented with their must in contact with the skins and seeds. Once the wine has extracted enough colour and tannin, which is a lot less for lighter wines from pinot noir and grenache than for the more full-bodied bruisers from shiraz and durif, the fermenting juice is pressed to separated from the skins – also to free run and pressings fractions.

Tannins and colour are very important for red wines, and the pressings, having more of these, can be blended back into the free run. After pressing, the juice is left to finish fermenting, now that it's a true red colour. Once fermentation has finished, we can call it wine.

Many red wines are left 'on their skins' for up to three or four weeks after fermentation, to achieve a better balance and richness by retaining softer tannins from the skins. These wines are fully dry by the time they are pressed.

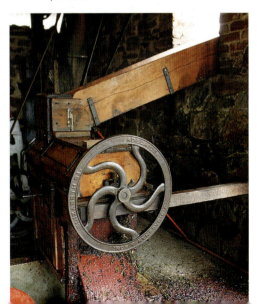

FINISHING THE WINE

By the time the yeast has converted the grape sugar to alcohol, a layer of grape and yeast deposit (or 'lees') will have settled at the bottom of the vessel containing the fermented wine. With reds, you might also have debris from skins and seeds. The wine needs to be syphoned off this layer in a process called 'racking', the term given to the process of moving clear juice or wine from on top of a deposit. This can happen several times during the winemaking process, and helps keep the wine fresh, vibrant and free from unwanted off odours.

After the yeast fermentation, the winemaker may permit the wine to ferment again, this time by bacteria. This secondary or malolactic fermentation converts malic acid (think of green apples) to lactic acid (a dairy acid so think of yoghurt this time), which is less acidic and 'softens out' many wines. All fermentations produce carbon dioxide gas (CO_2) and this is no exception. Virtually all red wines undergo a secondary fermentation before bottling, to avoid it taking place accidentally inside the bottle, by strange and unwelcome bugs. Such an event would ruin the wine's flavour as well as its clarity by leaving an unwelcome bacterial haze in the bottle.

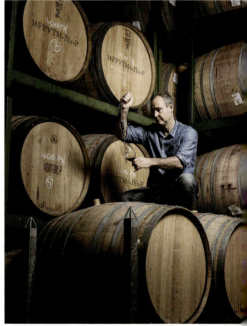

THE ROLE OF OAK BARRELS

Many wines, especially reds, are matured for a period in oak casks before bottling. While in wood, wines undergo a slow and controlled oxidation, which with the natural flavour pick-up from the oak, adds greatly to their complexity. Oak contributes a variety of flavours and characters, usually giving more depth and weight to the wine. Frequently the flavours bear no resemblance to oak at all. Biscuity, buttery, lemony, vanillin, toasty, coconut-like and even bubblegum-like flavours can be the result of oak maturation, all of which can ultimately contribute to wine's complexity and quality.

Most of the best barrels are made from European oaks, particularly from France. Oaks from different countries impart their own distinct flavours and properties. Winemakers can regulate the amount of oak character in their wines by understanding that young barrels impart more character to wine than older ones, small barrels more than large, and the longer a wine is in barrel the more 'oaked' it gets.

Many labels proclaim that their contents were matured in 100% new oak. This is a flashy, but risky process, since it is so easy for 100% brand-new oak to dominate the fruit in wine. The more conventional process is to use one-third each of brand new, one year-old and two year-old. The wines that are truly able to handle 100% new oak are those with profound layers of depth, flavour and structure.

Maturing wine in brand-new small oak casks is very expensive, for small new casks from France cost many hundreds of dollars. Today many Australian wineries produce handsomely oaked wines at affordable prices by inserting oak planks, staves or shavings into stainless steel tanks holding the wine, in much the same way that tea is made from tea leaves. This is rapid and infinitely cheaper. Although it cannot imitate the true wood ageing of oak casks completely, it can be very difficult to identify if used carefully.

CREATING SPARKLING WINE

The traditional 'Methode Champenoise' is today used around the world, and in many Australian wine regions, especially the cooler ones, to create delicious sparkling wines. When you see these words on a label, you know the contents of the bottle got their fizz the same way as the French put the gas into Gosset.

A Benedictine monk by the name of Don Pérignon observed how to get the bubbles into the bottle, while a venerable widow, Madame Veuve Clicquot, demanded that her staff figured out how to get the dead yeast out.

Step one is to make a white wine, fermented bone-dry. Dissolve in some sugar, add a carefully selected yeast and bottle it in the process of 'tirage'. The wine ferments all over again, but this time the CO_2 gas is trapped inside the bottle, giving all those wonderful bubbles and yet more alcohol. After some time, a large deposit or 'lees' of dead is left in the bottle, which needs to be removed before the wine is put up for sale.

By gradually twisting and turning the bottles over a period of time in special racks or 'Champagne tables', so that they finish by sitting upside-down, the sediment gathers behind the seal. This process is called 'riddling' or the 'remuage', and is carried out by highly-

skilled craftsmen, called 'remeurs' in Champagne, who deftly go about this responsible operation at amazing speed. These days most companies use a machine called a gyropalette, which is a large efficient machine able to replicate this process exactly.

Once all the sediment has gathered on the inside end of the cork, the neck of the bottle is rapidly frozen, and the cork or seal removed. The plug blasts out of the bottle, in explosive fashion, in the process of 'disgorging'.

The level in the bottle is now a little low, and has to be replenished. The wine inside is exceptionally dry – after all, it has been fermented twice. This final step before corking determines the style of the wine in a single step. Even the very driest of sparkling wines, which are labelled 'Brut' (meaning dry), receive a shot of sweetened wine before corking, except for a rare few called 'Natur Brut' or 'Brut Sauvage' (wild).

Sweeter, or 'demi-sec' wines are made by adding more sugar in the wine used to top up the bottles, called the 'liqueur d'expidition'. Sparkling wines, incidentally, are the only style of table wine allowing the deliberate addition of sugar in this or any other way. By choosing the 'taché' method, which involves adding a shot of red wine to the liqueur, you can turn the product pink, into a sparkling rosé.

SPARKLING WINE QUALITY

is profoundly affected by the time the wine spends inside the bottle between the second fermentation and disgorging, while in contact with the decaying yeast cells, which makes another deposit, or lees. The longer this period, the more yeast character in the wine, up to a point. Yeastiness is often likened to meaty and bready, doughy flavours, but in spite of this it is extremely pleasant and is the hallmark of a great wine.

The better vintage sparkling wines (made from grapes harvested in a single year) typically experience more than two years in contact with the yeast lees. In France, vintage Champagne is required to spend three years, which is a model usually adopted for Australia's finest wines, some of which are matured in this fashion for even longer.

FORTIFIED WINES

Fortified wines are made by adding alcoholic spirit to table wines either during or after their fermentation. Sweet fortified wines, some Australian muscat styles for example, are made by adding the alcohol, as neutral grape-spirit (or brandy in the more expensive cases) to the wine when it has fermented to the desired level of sweetness. The spirit immediately kills the yeast and stops the fermentation at that point. Dry fortifieds are made by adding the spirit to wines after they have fermented dry. Fortified wines typically must contain at least 17 percent alcohol by volume, and many contain much more. Therefore, they are appreciably stronger than table wines, and are usually enjoyed in much smaller glasses.

Most Australian fortified wine is a blend across vintages young and old, typically matured in very large and very old wooden casks. Australian wineries, particularly those in warmer regions, have historically made a wide range of fortified wines. Some are remarkably similar to the sherries from Spain, being made in a range of very dry to very sweet, while others are very much of Australia's own invention. These include luscious sweet wines from the muscat varieties in regions like Rutherglen and Griffith, as well as ancient oak-matured old fortified shiraz wines from the Barossa and McLaren Vale.

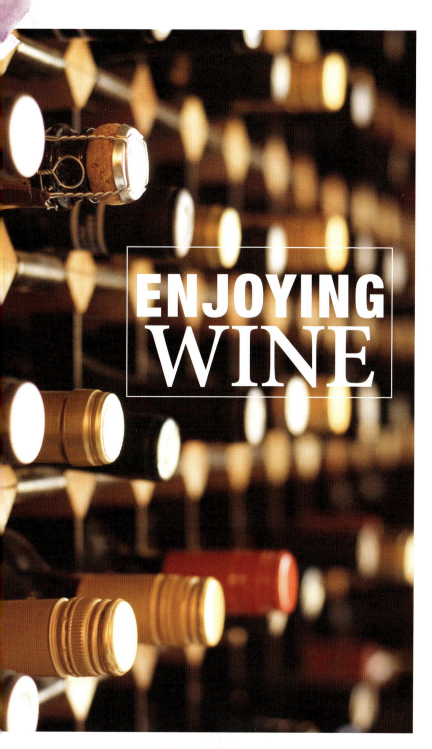

ENJOYING WINE

TASTING WINE

NO DOUBT YOU HAVE SEEN THE RITUAL: PEOPLE SWIRLING, SNIFFING AND SPITTING ALL THE WHILE APPARENTLY LOST IN A WORLD OF THEIR OWN. STRANGELY, THERE IS ACTUALLY A SOLID BASE OF SCIENCE BEHIND THE PROCESS OF TASTING WINE PROFESSIONALLY. FOLLOW THESE STEPS AND YOU'LL LEARN HOW.

1 CHOOSE A CLEAR GLASS, preferably shaped like a tulip and without cuts or grooves. Grab it by the stem - that way the bowl stays clear and you won't warm wines above their serving temperature with the heat of your hand. Fill your glass to its widest point (actually very low for a tasting glass) and you're ready to go.

2 TAKE A LOOK AT THE WINE BY TILTING YOUR GLASS AGAINST A WHITE BACKGROUND, preferably in a well-lit place. The colours in the wine should now be easier to detect. White wines tend to begin life with a green colour, after which with age they move to straw and then yellow, finally to a yellow-amber and brown, by which stage it is usually time to return them to the earth from whence they came. Wood-matured whites often show a more advanced colour, resulting from the slow and controlled oxidation they experience in oak casks, which is a form of ageing itself.

Reds begin purple, moving to purple-red, red, red-brown, and finally to that tawny brown, usually suggesting that it well and truly arrived at maturity, or perhaps beyond...

3 **NOW TAKE A SNIFF.** Hold the glass by its stem and swirl the wine around once or twice. Put your nose right inside and take a large sniff before the wine has stopped moving. Isn't that more intense?

The smell of wine can be divided into those flavours derived from its 'grapiness' or 'aroma', and those flavours which result from the wine's own development and change in the bottle as it ages. New aromatic compounds, collectively known as the 'bouquet', are formed as flavours break down and recombine within the wine.

Young wines show a dominance of 'aroma', while older, very developed wines can reveal almost 100% bouquet. The aromas and bouquets of classic grape varieties, like cabernet sauvignon and riesling, are remarkably consistent from wine to and can become quite identifiable to the taster.

As wine ages, its bouquet becomes less obvious and more intriguing as different components merge together in a harmonious way. With excessive age, it goes flat, loses its quality and can acquire a dull, toffee-like bouquet.

Your nose will also detect a range of winemaking faults. Smells of decaying vegetables, old socks, burnt rubber, horse hair, onion-skins or foreign objects often signal disaster. Some faults are tolerated a little more than others, largely because different people have different threshold level to different smells, while some of us are more tolerant of slight imperfections if the overall result is pleasing enough.

ALCOHOL IS IMPORTANT TO THE TASTE OF WINE

Alcohol, which typically accounts for between 10-14.5% of the volume of wine, makes an important contribution to its taste and mouthfeel. Take the alcohol out of wine, which several modern techniques can do, and it's typically thin and lacking richness and presence on the palate. On the other hand, if wines are made with 15% or more of alcohol, it then usually makes a strong, undeniable and entirely unwanted contribution to the taste and texture of different wines that tends to destroy their sense of harmony and balance. In such cases, alcohol contributes a spirity warmth more suggestive of a liqueur or fortified wine. Its influence is impossible to ignore.

4 **FINALLY, HAVE A TASTE.** Do this with confidence and a degree of aggression. Take a good mouthful of wine; there's no sense in mucking around with a polite sip. Purse your lips slightly and suck in a little air, which will evaporate volatile wine flavours and shoot them up to the olfactory centre underneath your brain, which is where you detect smell. Once again, it's like turning up the intensity of flavour.

The ability of your mouth to detect flavour is extremely restricted, and most of the perception of wine flavour takes place as I have just described. Apart from being able to detect hot and cool flavours like curry and mint, the tongue can only distinguish five basic tastes: sweetness at its tip, saltiness at its front sides, acidity along the sides, bitterness across the back and the savoury or 'umami' taste.

Fruit flavours are generally perceived towards the front of the mouth, where you can also detect if the wine is sweet or dry. Acidity and sweetness are frequently capable of rendering the other less noticeable, often to the point when you wonder if the other is there at all.

It's easily possible to mistake a wine's fruitiness for sweetness.

Acid is essential in all wine – for in addition to the freshness and tang it gives to round off flavour, it is also a preservative against microbial spoilage. Wines lacking in acid taste fat, flabby and overly broad, before falling away and finishing short in the mouth. Think of acid as the punctuation that finishes the taste.

Structure in wine, easily noticed in red wines as the tannins that pucker up the inside of your mouth, are usually picked up from the skins, stalks and seeds of grapes, while some can be extracted from oak casks. White wines made with skin contact prior to fermentation can also have texture and leave a physical impression on your palate. Wine tannins are virtually identical to those found in certain teas and have the same effect on your palate.

Wines should deliver some impact from the front of the palate – around your teeth – all the way along the palate to the back of your tongue. Furthermore, the flavour should persist after the wine has been swallowed or, if it's the expected protocol, spat out. This means it has length of flavour.

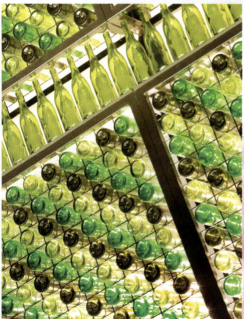

5. A CLOSING THOUGHT.

Finally, you should be left with the impression that all of the different facets of the wine, both textural and flavour-related, are in some form of harmony and balance. As such, there shouldn't be any single feature, such as oak tannin or acid for instance, which over-dominates any other. Fruit is a legitimate exception to this and there's no issue if it takes centre stage. Fine wines represent a harmonious balance of their various components. Although they might seem rather firm and tannic to drink at a young age, even traditional Australian cellaring shiraz and cabernet sauvignon must be in excellent balance not only to survive, but actually to improve over time.

HOW TO SERVE WINE

THE CORRECT TEMPERATURE TO SERVE WINE

Most us realise that whites should be drunk chilled and reds should be enjoyed at or just below room temperature, but let's think a bit more deeply. Most white wine is actually served over-chilled. That's because we live in a world without many wine fridges, but with a plethora of beer fridges and food fridges. So, most of the time, if we take out of a fridge a bottle of wine that has been there for some considerable time, it will be too cold.

The danger of serving a wine too cool is that the colder the wine, the less its flavours are able to evaporate. Our perception of flavour depends on a wine's ability to deliver volatile flavour molecules and on our ability to detect them. Over-chilled wines appear aroma-less, tasteless and bland. The most vulnerable white wines are usually from the less aromatic varieties like chardonnay, semillon and arneis, plus the richer and broader varieties like viognier and roussanne. More aromatic white wines from grapes such as riesling, gewürztraminer and sauvignon blanc can handle more of a chill, especially if they're made in a dry, racy and refreshing style.

The effervescence of sparkling wines assists their retention of aroma and flavour at low temperatures, so they can be opened cooler than other wines.

The only reds I'd ever chill - which is not to be confused with bringing down to room temperature or below with a brief spell in the refrigerator - are the lighter, more aromatic reds made without much tannin – like Beaujolais for instance – or some of the modern lighter wines made from southern Rhône varieties of grenache, shiraz and mourvèdre.

BREATHING AND DECANTING

Wine is decanted for two purposes: to help separate the wine from a deposit or sediment that might have accumulated over time in the bottle, and to open up its bouquet and palate through a gentle process of aeration or 'breathing'.

Mature red wines might have accumulated a deposit of sediment, fine or coarse, over time. This is a precipitation of the acids, tannins and colours that occur quite naturally in wine and is no cause for concern. The main issue is how to enjoy the wine without having to sift your way through a glass full of such deposit.

If there's enough sediment that might make pouring a wine difficult, you will need to stand the bottle upright for an hour or more – enough time in fact for all the sediment to fall to the bottom, making a layer at the base of the bottle. The finer the sediment, the longer this will take. In all but the rarest of cases, three or four hours is as long as you will need.

Then, once you begin to remove the cork or take off the screwcap, it's vital that you keep the bottle upright, so not to send the deposit of sediment back into suspension.

A COUPLE OF DECANTING TIPS.

One is to use a wine filter if you haven't had the time to leave the bottle upright for long enough, or if you're at all unsure. You can even use a coffee filter paper, if nothing else is at hand! Tip two is to place a small torch or even a candle beneath the neck of the bottle as you are pouring, which helps give you a clear view if any sediment is about to be poured out as well as the clear wine.

Pour the wine very slowly and carefully into a clean glass vessel, such as a jug, a carafe or better still, a decanter. It's important to watch the wine entering the jug or decanter through the neck of the bottle, so you can stop pouring the moment you observe the sediment about to be poured in as well as the wine.

When you decant a bottle of wine, you are also aerating the wine as well. This is known as 'breathing', and it can perform a couple of useful tasks. Firstly, an old wine may contain some slightly pungent or 'off' characters which can dissipate into the atmosphere and out of the wine.

The second thing that happens is that oxygen is able to get to the wine, and through a slight oxidation process is able to sharpen the edge on many of its flavours, enhancing their attraction and depth. So, as a wine breathes, it improves with the loss of undesirable flavours, while its 'winey' flavours are made more apparent to the drinker. You do it simply by leaving the wine open for a period prior to drinking - in a jug, carafe or decanter.

Decanting also helps to accelerate the breathing process in younger and more robust wines, which, being more resilient, are acceptably able to submit to a harsher treatment. By pouring them alternately from one decanter or carafe to another, you thereby impose a gentle, extended and effective process of aeration. There is however a danger with old wine. If you breathe it for too long, it can rapidly oxidise and deteriorate, losing its remaining freshness of flavour. You need to balance one outcome against the other.

SIMPLY LEAVING AN OPENED BOTTLE

standing upright will never replicate proper breathing. The surface area of the exposed wine in the bottle is simply far too small to permit anything other than minuscule evaporation and dissolving of oxygen, especially when compared to the comparatively broad expanse of wine's surface inside a decanter. Decanting gives wine a gentle aeration, reducing the time required for it to breathe to its most drinkable degree.

KEEPING UNFINISHED BOTTLES OF WINE

Don't go and buy hand-held vacuum pumps and the like – they do more harm than good in my view. It's actually a simple and inexpensive process. Similarly, don't waste your money on cans of inert gas that purport to displace oxygen. They will send you broke.

One options is to reseal the bottle with a clean cork and put it into the refrigerator to slow its rate of oxidation. Then, if it's a red wine, just leave it outside the refrigerator for long enough to warm back up to around 18 degrees Celsius before serving. This works surprisingly well.

Or you can pour the remaining contents into a clean 375 ml wine bottle (a half bottle) and re-cork it. You can then refrigerate this bottle to help it last even longer. It involves a little more work, but is by far the best thing you can do. Easy.

THE RULES OF DECANTING:

1. Young reds generally need longer to breathe than old ones, and full-bodied reds need longer than more delicate wines.

2. A long period of breathing is around three hours; a short period about fifteen minutes.

3. Therefore, give a full-bodied young wine the full three hours, and delicate older, ones about fifteen minutes or more, depending on how they smell when opened.

4. Old wines (20 years of age and more) should be opened around half an hour before they are ready to be drunk. Once opened, immediately sniff the top of the bottle. If it smells sweet and fragrant, the screwcap should be resealed or cork should re-inserted (the same way as before). A clean cork might be needed instead. These wines will not require that half-hour's breathing.

WHAT DO WE DO WHEN ASKED TO INSPECT AND TASTE A WINE IN A RESTAURANT?

The idea is to determine whether or not the wine has been affected by its cork, its storage or is otherwise spoiled by a significant wine fault. Given that restaurants should not list flawed wines and that most Australian wine is sealed with a screwcap, this process is virtually redundant.

However, if a wine is sealed by a cork it carries risk that cork failure might (i) affect the aroma and taste of a wine and (ii) lead to premature aging and spoilage.

The most commonly detected problem that cork causes is to impart a smell and taste similar to mouldy wet cardboard into the wine, most likely the result of a chemical called 2,4,6 trichloroanisole (or TCA). While there are also other cork taints, such as a less-common woody cork taste, perhaps the most damaging effect of cork taint is that it dulls wine flavour and diminishes the enjoyment it provides.

More common is the phenomenon presently known as 'random oxidation'. It's a result of air entering the wine, either through or around the cork. Again, at low levels, this can simply dull the wine, and in such cases, most people would not be confident enough to request another bottle. At higher levels, random oxidation can however produce strong toffee-like or brown (cut) apple smells, not unlike sherry or madeira. Very low-level incidences of this are also the most damaging, since they can make bottles taste disappointing without actually providing a detectable reason why.

CELLARING WINE

HOW WINE MATURES

It's quite understandable that many people make a basic misapprehension about the way wine alters with time. Wine doesn't simply become a more intense or expressive version of what it might have been while in its youth, but it actually evolves, undergoing sometimes dramatic changes in colour, smell and taste.

The process of ageing is one of the most complex and least understood of all aspects of wine appreciation. Involving the polymerisation between the many types of molecule present in young wine, it commences as a slow and controlled oxidation before becoming a reductive maturation in older wine.

As wines mature, their constituent components of fruit, oak, tannin and acidity alter and marry together, hopefully in a harmonious and pleasing way. Complex volatile esters form when acids combine with ethanol (the alcohol in wine), while aldehydes form as ethanol is itself oxidised. Ultimately, this esterification reduces and softens the occasionally tart acidity found in young wine.

Just as their colours become deeper and darker with time, the palate of white wines firstly becomes richer and rounder, before sliding towards an inevitable decay. Excessive maturation is illustrated by a shortening of the wine's impact on your palate as its acid level drops below desirable levels, an over-dominance of oxidised characters resembling toffee, brown apples and vinegar and a loss of desirable fruit intensity.

While some pinot noirs will 'build' in the bottle over their first two years in glass, most red wines begin a gradual process of refinement and ever-increasing restraint as they mature. With reds, bottle age and development is closely linked to the polymerisation of wine tannins, themselves polymers of polyphenols extracted from grape skins and the insides of oak barrels.

As they combine, molecules that were once relatively small become very large in older wines, reducing their ability to impact with the proteins in the mouth and create the familiar puckering astringency we associate with wine tannin. As they polymerise, polyphenols and tannins may frequently combine with colour and acid, creating crusts or sediment in maturing wine. As wines become older, their ability to impart a discernible effect from tannin reduces and they become noticeably softer and smoother to drink.

HOW TO CELLAR WINE

If it's sealed with a cork keep your wine upside down or on its side. While some scientists suggest that the partial pressure of water between the wine's surface and the cork in an upright bottle is enough to keep the cork sufficiently moist, I'm not prepared to take the risk. If corks dry out, air gets in. This is ruinous. An added advantage wines packaged with screwcap seals for longevity and to guard against cork taint is that you can actually cellar them upright without concern. I have am amazed at the improved ability of both whites and reds to mature with these seals.

Keep your wine in the dark. Ultra-violet light can penetrate most glass bottles to some degree (especially the clear ones) and oxidise the wine inside. This is why so many cellars

A BIG TIP:

Regardless of its actual colour, you hope the appearance of the old wine you're opening is bright, glistening and still able to reflect light. The alternative is that it might look dull and flat, in which in case it's likely to have lost too much acidity. This typically causes the wine to 'break', lose freshness and flavour and dry out from the back of the palate.

are dimly lit. If you haven't the space for a dark cellar, keep your bottles in their boxes or else behind a heavy curtain.

Keep your wine still and undisturbed. Regular vibrations accelerate the ageing process with wine. Furthermore, there's no need to turn your bottles every morning, as some people regularly do. This habit began when English gentlemen needed an unobtrusive means of checking that their household staff hadn't secreted any away from their premises, so they actually did this to count their stock.

Temperature should be both constant and low. There is debate about the ideal cellaring temperature. In my experience, if wine is cellared above 18 degrees Celsius it ages too quickly. If it is cellared at around 10–12 degrees, it ages very slowly, perhaps too slowly for some of us. Around 14 degrees is probably ideal, which means that in most parts of Australia, you will need some temperature control. Most importantly, changes in temperature from day to night and from season to season must be avoided if wine is to be kept for even a few months. So, keep wine well away from windows and external walls, unless they're very thick.

Think about humidity. If a cellar is too humid then labels and racks may go mouldy. It's unlikely that the wines themselves will be adversely affected, but it's not worth the risk with rare and expensive wines. If there's not enough humidity in the cellar, the outward ends of wine corks may shrink and reduce their ability to impart a seal. This can considerably shorten a wine's longevity. A bowl of water, or even water tipped onto a gravel floor (ideal!!), can help.

A REDUCTION IN THE ACTUAL VOLUME OF WINE

in the bottle (or 'ullage') is to expected with very mature wines. Bottles with less ullage are likely to be in better condition than the same wines whose ullage is more pronounced. The greater the ullage, the more oxygen admitted into the bottle, the greater the consequent risk of wine spoilage through oxidation. Seasonal changes in temperature alternately create a positive and negative pressures inside the bottle, expelling minute quantities of wine from the bottle in the process. Visible weeping from a bottle usually demands rapid attention.

IF YOU DON'T HAVE A CELLAR…

Think about a temperature and humidity-controlled wine cabinet. Then you won't have a worry in the world about the health of your wine or your ability to access it. Some of these units are particularly impressive. Take into account include your ability to change temperature settings, the ease of access to the wines inside, possible temperature zoning within the unit to provide different compartments for whites and reds, whether or not fresh air circulates throughout the unit, that the inside of the unit is dark, that it is lockable, that any glass doors are UV-treated, and that the degree of vibration caused by motor units is minimal.

Wine Australia

Wine Australia is part of The Australian Grape and Wine Authority, the Australian Government body that provides services to and for the Australian grape growing and wine industry.

Wine Australia is responsible for the government-backed promotion of Australian wine, both in Australia and overseas. It has offices in Australia, the United Kingdom, North America and China, each of which conduct market development programs that operate with wine companies either keen to enter or maintain their positions in that market. Much of Wine Australia's current overseas marketing activity is conducted in conjunction with Tourism Australia and the various State tourism authorities.

Jeremy Oliver has a long history of working with Wine Australia and has conducted promotional events for this body in Australia, Singapore, Japan, China and the US. Recently, the Beijing office of Wine Australia was closely involved in the launch of the Chinese language edition of Jeremy Oliver's 2016 The Australian Wine Annual.

Jeremy would like to acknowledge the role of Wine Australia in providing many of the illustrations presented in this book.

Wine Australia

Your own notes...